first
you
have
to
row
a
little
boat

.

first you have to row a little boat

REFLECTIONS ON LIFE & LIVING

RICHARD BODE

WARNER BOOKS

A Time Warner Company

Warner Books, Inc., 1271 Avenue of the Americas,
New York, NY 10020

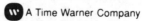 A Time Warner Company

Printed in the United States of America
First Printing: May 1993
10 9 8 7 6 5 4

Library of Congress Cataloging-in-Publication Data

Bode, Richard.
    First you have to row a little boat : Reflections on life and
living / Richard Bode.
        p.   cm.
    ISBN 0-446-51681-3
    1. Spiritual life.   2. Sailing.   3. Bode, Richard.   I. Title.
BL624.B59   1993
818′.5403—dc20
[B]   92-50528
                                                           CIP

Book design by Giorgetta Bell McRee

For Bonnie
Who makes all things possible

CONTENTS

·

first
you
have
to
row
a
little
boat
.

ONE

·

THE MARINER'S RHYME

·

When I was a young man I made a solemn vow. I swore I would teach my children to sail. It was a promise never kept.

The exigencies of life—money, work, location, and health—kept me from passing on to my children this legacy which I deem to be the essence of myself. I feel as if I have left something unsaid which I ought to have said, something undone which I ought to have done. I am filled with a lore which I learned as a boy, and I failed to pass it on to my sons and daughters, who will now fail to pass it on to theirs.

I try to forgive myself, but I can't. No matter how many excuses I make, I am faced with the unalterable fact: I did not teach my children to sail.

In my mind's eye, in the quiet night, in my vagrant dreams, I see myself doing what I didn't do. I take my children out one by one in the tender sloop I sold soon after they were born. I teach them to sail out the saltwater creek and to point for the lighthouse across the bay. I teach them to bring the bow or the stern across the face of the wind: to tack or jibe. I teach them to raise or lower the sails, to throw an anchor overboard, to bring the boat up to a mooring in a heavy sea. Through it all I know I am not merely teaching them to sail. I am showing them, hopefully without the taint of preachment, that they are engaged in a metaphor. To sail a boat is to negotiate a life— that is what I want them to understand.

Yet I confess that when I learned to sail as a youth, I had no idea that the lessons of simple seamanship had such universal application and would stand me in such good stead later on. I didn't sense a wind shift and say to myself, Aha, there's another one of life's little lessons. I tacked, jibed, drifted, anchored; I adjusted myself to the conditions I

found. I was enjoying myself and acquiring a skill—
that's what I thought.

What I didn't know was that I was also developing
a consciousness, an acute awareness of the relationship between myself and the elements over which I
had no control. God gave the wind. It might blow
from the east, west, north, or south. It might gust;
it might fall off to practically nothing. It might leave
me dead becalmed. I didn't pick the wind; that was
imposed by a power far greater than myself. But I
had to sail the wind—against it, with it, sideways
to it; I had to wait it out with the patience of Job
when it didn't blow—if I wanted to move myself
from where I was to where I wanted to go.

As humans we live with the constant presumption
of dominion. We believe that we own the world,
that it belongs to us, that we have it under our firm
control. But the sailor knows all too well the fallacy
of this view. The sailor sits by his tiller, waiting and
watching. He knows he isn't sovereign of earth and
sky, any more than the fish in the sea or the birds
in the air. He responds to the subtle shiftings of
the wind, the imperceptible ebbings of the tide. He
changes course. He trims his sheets. He sails.

The hurricane, the typhoon, the tsunami, the sudden squall—they are all sharp reminders of the puni-
ness of man when measured against the momentous
forces of nature. We aren't in total charge of our
fate. We are subject to death, accident, and disease;
we can, without warning, lose love, work, home.

3
•
first
you
have
to
row
a
little
boat

An unseen hand can rise at any moment from an unexpected quadrant of the compass and strike us down.

I lost both my parents to death—first my father and then my mother—while I was still a boy. That was a colossal storm, an irreversible wind that changed my destiny. I didn't command that wind and I couldn't make it give back what it had taken away. But it was my wind and I had to sail it until it led me at last to a sheltered cove.

All that happened to me a half century ago, and I have survived. In the intervening years I have discovered that—despite the overwhelming nature of that early disaster—day-to-day life isn't a constant series of crises and calamities. Day-to-day life is like the wind in all its infinite variations and moods. The wind is shifting, constantly shifting, blowing north northeast, then northeast, then north—just as we, ourselves, are constantly shifting, sometimes happy, sometimes angry, sometimes sad. As the sailor sails his winds, so we must sail our moods.

I find myself sharing these thoughts with my children as we sail together through my mythical dreams. But we didn't sail together and so I never told them—and maybe it's just as well. If the condition of fatherhood has taught me one thing, it is the difficulty, if not utter impossibility, of passing on to my offspring the lessons of my separate life. I found out, almost after it was too late, that my children weren't born to learn from my experiences; they were born to learn from their own, and any attempt on my part to substitute my perceptions for theirs was doomed to fail.

The truth is that, for all my sorrow and regret, I can't go on forever condemning myself for what I did or didn't do. I learned to sail when I was a youth and my children did not—and that is the sum of it. I don't know why that happened anymore than I know why some students head straight for the school library and others for the gym. I suspect there are destinations that call to us from a secret place within ourselves and we head for them instinctively.

The silent currents within my own life led me down to the sea in a sailboat when I was still a boy. That was the course I chose for myself—and it has made all the difference in my life and memory.

My children are grown now and involved in their own lives, with their own distinctive triumphs and discoveries, and I am left with a tale untold and no one to tell it to. And so what I write now is in its way an expiation for the sins of omission I committed in the past. I am like the Ancient Mariner, seizing innocent stragglers and wayward passersby and telling them my rhyme.

5
•
first
you
have
to
row
a
little
boat

TWO

·

THE FIRST THING YOU HAVE TO DO IS LEARN TO ROW A LITTLE BOAT

·

The urge to sail first came upon me when I was twelve. I stood on the shore and watched the boats dipping, righting themselves, and dipping again in the onshore breeze. It seemed like such a simple sport, far easier than hitting a home run or shooting an oversize ball through a metal hoop. I thought all I had to do was raise the canvas, let it fill with wind, and the boat and I would take off together like a soaring bird. But the first man to get me off the land and into a boat had a decidedly different idea.

His name was Harrison Watts, and in the beginning I knew him only by reputation. He was a legendary sailor who had skippered racing sloops and iceboats as far back as the turn of the century when the Great South Bay froze over every winter from the Long Island mainland clear to the Fire Island Light. If you go down to the end of Ocean Avenue in the old seaside town of Bay Shore, you will find the captain's wood-frame house still standing there, just north of the boat basin, backing on the busy saltwater creek. For all I know, you may also find his stubby charter boat, the *Nimrod*—which he ran before, during, and after World War II—sitting at her berth, swaying in the wind, even though the captain himself has been dead these many years. He has gone the way of his forebears, the early settlers of this far eastern shore, who were whalers and seafarers right down to their rheumatic bones.

I saw the captain often, albeit from a respectful distance, because he berthed the *Nimrod* across a narrow waterway from the shipyard where I spent most of my spare time. He was a portly man of about seventy with a cherubic face which he kept shaded by a white canvas cap with a long bill; despite a gimpy gait he moved from the dock to the deck

9
•
first
you
have
to
row
a
little
boat

of his boat and back to the dock again with catlike agility. He would appear regularly at the *Nimrod*'s helm on summer afternoons, returning from the bay with a fishing party aboard, chugging up the creek, towing a snub-nosed dinghy behind. He saw me, too, I'm sure, because I was always sitting on the bulkhead, waiting for his arrival so I could observe the easy way he maneuvered his boat into her slip.

He became my mentor in the most natural way. It was late June, school was out, and the long summer vacation had just begun. I arrived at the shipyard early one morning, braced my bike against a boat shed, and as I came around the side of the dilapi-dated building I saw the *Nimrod* hauled clear out of the water, up on the ways, with the captain under-neath flat on his back, scraping her bottom. I ap-proached him with apprehension, for he was still part myth to me and I thought he might rise like a sea god and bite off my head. I settled on a huge wooden block beside his boat, and when he finally turned and spoke to me I realized that my fears were unfounded. He was only a man, and an amiable one at that.

"So, my boy," he said as if we were the best of friends, "what brings you down here so early in the day?"

"I'm looking for a boat," I said. It wasn't the exact truth, but it wasn't a total fabrication, either.

"What sort of boat?"

"A sailboat."

"Can you sail?"

It was a question I dreaded, for one of the hardest things in life is to confess ignorance when trying to impress. I could deceive my friends; in fact, I often did with idle tales about what I would do and where I would go if I owned a boat of my own, and they looked at me as one who knew exactly what he was talking about. At the age of twelve, it's extremely difficult to resist the adulation of one's peers. But the captain was a different matter. He was the master of an ancient art form I wanted to possess, and I knew he would see through my pretensions right away.

"No, I can't," I said.

"Have you ever been in a sailboat?"

"Not really."

"You've never sailed. You've never even been in a sailboat. Yet you want to get yourself a boat. How do you figure that?"

"Oh, I guess I'll manage."

He rolled out from under the *Nimrod* and pulled himself up straight. I honestly expected at that moment he was going to conjure up a tidy sloop in which he and I would sail away. But there was to be no sailing lesson that day. Instead, he reached into the cockpit of his boat, pulled out a couple of oars, and walked down to the snub-nosed dinghy he had tied up against the dock. He handed me the oars.

"Get in!" he said. "The first thing you have to do is learn to row a little boat."

I looked at the dinghy; I doubt it was more than ten feet long. It sat there bobbing on the surface like a cork, an affront to my ego. I didn't want a rowboat; I wanted a sloop, a ketch, or a yawl. I wanted to sail the bay, cross the ocean, cruise the world.

11

•

first
you
have
to
row
a
little
boat

I stepped aboard, holding the oars, standing straight up; the rowboat lurched and almost pitched me into the drink. The captain said nothing; I guess he figured there were some things I would have to learn for myself.

For three consecutive days I rowed that dinghy back and forth across the creek, about two hundred yards from bulkhead to bulkhead, dodging clam boats, ferries, and pleasure craft. Occasionally, the captain would walk out to the end of the dock, wave me ashore, and offer a few helpful hints, but most of the time he stood there quietly, watching me pull at the oars. Was he pleased with my progress? I like to think he was. But I know this: I was pleased with myself, for I was mastering a milieu entirely different from any I had ever known before.

Hour by hour, day by day, under the captain's silent tutelage, I acquired a skill which, as much as walking or talking, remains fundamental to my view of the world. First, I learned to pull both oars together, then I learned I could also propel the boat forward at a different pace by alternating my strokes. I gained a new perspective on inertia, for the boat was hard to start, since it didn't have an engine, and harder to stop, since it didn't have a brake. It had but one motive source of power, and that was me.

We are creatures of the land and we respond to the conventions of the land. First, we learn to ride a tricycle, then a bicycle, and finally, when we come of age, we graduate to a car. But they all have one element in common: wheels that roll across unyielding surfaces of concrete or asphalt. Turn the wheels to the left and the vehicle veers to the left; to the right and it veers to the right. The convention of the wheel is ingrained in us at an early age and from that moment on we tend to apply it to virtually everything we do.

But the boat I rowed that day had no wheels and it didn't ride upon a hardened surface. It had a flat bottom that floated freely in a pliable sea, and it operated in a manner exactly opposite to a bike or a car. Pull on the left oar and the dinghy veered to the right; on the right oar and it veered to the left. Pull on one oar and push on the other and the boat turned sharply on its axis. All those motions were contrary to the ones I knew, and they called for a fundamental adjustment of muscle and mind.

The truth is that in our daily lives we constantly make similar migrations from land to water and back to land again—and we don't always do so with the fluency of the sailor. Time flips us rapidly from place to place and role to role. We shuttle from suburb to city, from home to job, from business meeting to dinner party. Each milieu has its own conventions and makes its own demands. Sometimes the changes occur so fast we lose our bearings. We behave like parents to our colleagues and executives to our kids. We lack a sure sense of the appropriate because we haven't taken the time to figure out where we are.

Few humans conduct their affairs with the aplomb of a duck, which is one sort of animal in the water and another in the air—and never confuses the two. In the former, it tucks back its wings and neck, extends its webbed feet, and paddles about, dunking or diving as it feeds. In the latter, it tucks back its feet, extends its neck, and unfolds its wings, beating them strongly as it flies.

I sat in the center of the dinghy, facing the stern, my destination somewhere behind me, a landfall I couldn't see. I had to judge where I was headed from where I had been, an acquired perception which has served me well—for the goals of my life, and especially my work, haven't always been visible points of light on a shore that looms in front of me. They are fixed in my imagination, shrouded and indistinct, and I detect them best when my eyes are closed. All too often I am forced to move toward them backward, like a boy in a rowboat, guiding myself by a cultivated inner sense of direction which tells me I'm on course, tending toward the place I want to be.

And so in time the rowboat and I became one and the same—like the archer and his bow or the artist and his paint. What I learned wasn't mastery

13

•

first
you
have
to
row
a
little
boat

over the elements; it was mastery over myself, which is what conquest is ultimately all about. We take our children to Little League so they can learn the supposed benefits of teamwork and competition, by which we mean domination of others in sport as well as life. But in life, real life, we aren't pitted against one another; we are pitted against ourselves, and our victories are almost always the ones we forge alone. If we want to teach our children self-reliance, then we shouldn't take them to the diamond or gridiron. We should take them down to a river, a lake or a bay and let them learn to row a little boat.

THREE

·

"A BOY'S WILL IS
THE WIND'S WILL . . ."

·

Tsaw the blue sloop long before I knew she would be mine. I was standing on the bulkhead at the shipyard when she suddenly materialized, gliding up the saltwater creek with the wind behind her, white sails billowing, graceful as a swan. As she slid past, the standing helmsman pulled the tiller toward him, away from the sail; the boat swung in a broad arc across the creek, jibing in the gentle breeze, and headed toward the bay. In a moment she was gone, but her sheer wooden hull and her bright varnished decks, glistening in the morning sun, remained fixed in my mind and memory long after she disappeared.

I wanted the blue sloop, but I had no idea how I could make her mine. She was aloof, and the best I could do was admire her, the way a youth admires a lovely lady—secretly and from afar. What I didn't know is that we grow toward our desire in the same way a flower grows toward the sun. We gain our ends not through seizure but affinity. The boat and the boy, the boy and the boat, are drawn toward each other, and when the passion is strong enough there is no power in heaven or earth that can keep them apart.

In the days that followed, the blue sloop became the standard of elegance against which I measured every boat I saw. There was no other like her, and as I poked about the shipyard, examining the vessels in dry dock and in the water, watching the owners clamber aboard their fancy yachts and sail away, I played an imaginary game. I pretended I could summon up a preternatural power, a sort of djinni, who would say to me, "Pick out the one boat that appeals to you the most of all you've seen, and I will make her yours." Without hesitation I would pick the blue sloop that had blown out of nowhere on a summer wind.

It was a daydream, of course, an activity that our society, with its penchant for productive employment, scorns. "Stop daydreaming! Surely you can find something more useful to do with your time!" I can still feel the sting of that adult rebuke, snapping me out of my boyhood reverie. I heard that reprimand repeatedly from my teachers, my guardians, even the parents of my friends—all of whom seemed to be engaged in a grand conspiracy to keep me from slipping into my private world.

It was poor advice, as impossible to follow now as it was then (for the daydreaming boy is father to the daydreaming man). Longfellow was right: "A boy's will is the wind's will /And the thoughts of youth are long, long thoughts," and there is no admonition severe enough to dislodge the daydreams that fill a child's head. Rather than suppress those dreams, he should be ordered to obey them, for they are the true harbingers of his future self. They tell him who he is and what he wants and in which direction he should tend.

We ignore these visions at our peril, for—contrary to conventional wisdom—they aren't as idle as they seem. They arise from a distilled longing to join ourselves with the spirit of truth and beauty that lies latent in us all. More than we know, we crave the symbols of that union, for they empower us with

17

·

first
you
have
to
row
a
little
boat

life. And so it wasn't the blue sloop I yearned to possess so much as the idea of the sloop, which was, up to that moment, the most grace-filled object I had ever beheld.

I had a choice; I know that now. I could have smothered the dream, killed it off, and paid the physical penalty for that repression. At the very least I would have grown a huge wart at the end of my nose. Or I could have kept it firmly fixed in my mind's eye and moved inexorably toward it with whatever resources I found at my command. Looking back, I realize I had been following the latter course, even though it didn't seem all that clear to me at the time. I had gone to the shipyard and befriended the captain, who taught me to row a little boat, and now I was waiting . . . waiting . . . for a chance to test my newfound skill on that veritable sailing paradise, the Great South Bay.

I had a classmate who lived near the water; and when I told him Capt. Harrison Watts was "a personal friend of mine," I became an instant celebrity in his eyes. He invited me to go for a sail in his older brother's boat. It turned out to be a sailing dinghy, barely larger than the captain's rowboat; it had a single sail and it was extremely tipsy, even in light airs.

We took turns at the tiller. Sometimes we turned the boat over deliberately, more often by mistake. But I had, without realizing it, advanced closer to my dream. I was now out of the protected saltwater

19

•

first
you
have
to
row
a
little
boat

creek into the choppy bay, and rather than pulling on a pair of oars I was relying on the inherent power of the wind to propel me toward my goal.

I decided I had to own a boat of my own, any boat, and I thought about confessing this desire to my aunt and uncle, with whom I lived. But they weren't people of means and I didn't feel I could ask them to lay out a large sum of money for me. They knew I spent most of my spare time either talking about sailboats or actually sailing, but I was sure they would dismiss this hankering of mine to own a boat as an adolescent whim that would pass with time.

I misjudged them, for when the time was right they came to my aid in a way I never would have supposed. They didn't supply me with money; they supplied me with something better, the contractor who built their new house and who had a powerboat of his own. His name was Ed Doubrava, and I never tired of watching him measure boards and drive nails as the wooden frame of the house rose about him room by room, seemingly more by magic than design. A lean man with a weathered face and thinning gray hair, he moved with effortless grace despite a physical handicap, the result (I learned from my uncle) of a childhood disease.

While he was still a boy, he was stricken with polio, which affected the left side of his body, especially his arm. His left hand reached only as far as his waist, but the arm itself was fully developed from manual labor and its muscles bulged. When I first met him, his shortened arm was his most apparent physical characteristic, but as I got to know him better I hardly noticed it at all.

He spoke to me while he worked, sometimes enlisting my help. At first I carried two-by-fours, then he showed me how to nail siding and shingle the roof. Whenever the opportunity arose, I would tell him about my desire to sail, and he would nod knowingly, without comment. When the house was finished, he offered me a summer job as his "apprentice"—fixing up windblown dwellings that faced the Atlantic on the barrier beach.

We left Bay Shore at seven every morning and headed across the bay. Ed knew the channels and, when the tide was in, he knew the shortcuts across the shoals and flats—and he passed this knowledge on to me. I learned by the color of the water when it was safe to skim slowly over the sandbars and when it was wiser to take the longer way around.

Ed and I spent a week together, living aboard his boat, docked in an idyllic backwater called Oak Island while we straightened out a beach house that had been bowled over by a hurricane. One day after work he walked into the tall reeds beside the house and dragged out a leaky duck blind, which had been converted by its owner into a makeshift sailboat. While I stood staring in disbelief, he told me it was mine, a gift outright from a friend of his who had no use for it anymore.

21
•
first
you
have
to
row
a
little
boat

There was only one difficulty; the boat had a mast and a boom, but it didn't have a sail. I presented this problem to my aunt, who was an excellent seamstress. She cut up a couple of old bed sheets and stitched them together; they weren't as sturdy as Egyptian cotton, the preferred sailcloth of that day, but they fit the duck blind perfectly. And now I had a sailboat of my own.

First time out, Ed and I sailed the duck boat around Oak Island, a circumnavigation I shall never forget. We skimmed in two feet of water, so close to the marsh we could hear the salt wind rustling in the reeds. On the north side of the island, Ed pointed to a pair of slender birds with black backs and white forked tails gliding off the bow. "Scissor-bills," he said, squinting into the sun. "They were here when I was a kid. They've been here for a million years, I guess."

Thereafter, I sailed the boat alone. As the summer progressed, we moved from port to port along Fire Island, towing the converted duck blind behind. I sat on the stern, watching the way my sailboat plowed dutifully along, riding the powerboat's wake. As the summer waned it was apparent that I was ready for something more substantial than a duck blind—and by then my uncle was persuaded that he could safely, as he put it, "make an investment" in me.

The following spring Ed found a sloop at a boatyard on Bellport Bay, farther east on the Long Island shore. It was nineteen feet long; it had a centerboard that popped up and down (instead of a keel) and a good suit of sails. The price was right, about $350. My uncle wrote out a check; and as soon as the weather turned sufficiently warm, I sailed her home.

The boat was flawed; she had a round bottom and she wasted an enormous amount of energy wallowing like a hippopotamus instead of slicing like a seal. She wasn't the prettiest sight at anchor or the most efficient under sail, but she was mine and I sailed her for two years, either mastering her idiosyncrasies or learning to live with them.

During that period I saw the blue sloop many times, looming on the horizon off Fire Island, scudding past south shore beaches under lowering skies. She remained as elusive as ever, the phantom of my waking dreams. And then toward the end of the second summer with my roly-poly sloop, I unexpectedly came upon an ad in the *Bay Shore Sentinel:*

> 23-foot Timber Point sloop
> with bright decks and blue hull.
> Two suits of sails, plus spinna-
> ker. $1250 firm.

I showed the ad to my uncle (purely for his information, I told myself, not daring to raise my hopes), and I remember how he sat there studying it for an interminably long time. Finally, he asked, "How much do you think we can get for the boat you now have?"

23
•
first
you
have
to
row
a
little
boat

"Maybe five hundred," I replied. "And I have a hundred and fifty dollars saved from working with Ed."

"Well, well," he said, "why don't we go down to the shipyard and have a look at this Timber Point of yours."

We stood side by side, studying the blue hull chocked up on the shipyard ways. She was as lovely out of the water as in, with her copper-red bottom and sturdy keel exposed.

I could see that my uncle was concerned. "Some hunk of machinery," he said. "First time out, you'd better take somebody along who knows how to handle a boat this large."

All these circumstances—a school chum and his brother's sailboat, Ed and his friend's duck blind—may seem like coincidences, dumb luck, happenstance. I might just as easily have never asked my aunt to sew a sail for me or shown my uncle that newspaper ad. But I question that interpretation of events. I had taken a dream, clung to it, nurtured it, never let it go. That dream governed my youthful actions and ultimately transformed my life.

I kept the blue sloop in a long canal bordered by a road on either side, and I would be less than honest if I didn't admit I took a certain pride of ownership. I was always pleased when motorists slowed down to admire the boat, especially when I was aboard, raising the sails, casting away. But if the boat was merely an adornment, like a piece of jewelry or a fancy hat, then it would hardly have been worth the dream.

No, the boat was more than its wood hull, lead keel, and canvas sails. The boat was the realization of that inner vision of wind, water, tides, terns, and salt air; it was the summation, the epiphany of a boy's life as it was, as it would become, as it had to be. The boat was not ersatz, not a plastic shell; it was authentic, the essence of life itself, the life I craved, the life that rose within me and would not die unless I died myself, every hour, every day, a little at a time.

When we kill the dream within us, we kill ourselves, even though the blood continues to flow within our veins. We can see the signs of this living death about us everywhere: in shopping malls, in discount and department stores, in frantic Christmas crowds. We see people scurrying compulsively, buying compulsively, as if they hoped through the expenditure of money, the acquisition of goods, to deaden a pain they don't even know they have.

I know a couple who uses shopping to dispel an unyielding sadness that seems to overwhelm them day by day. Whenever their depression becomes more than they can bear, they buy new furniture for their living room. And it helps—for a while. But in due course the sadness engulfs them again, and they don't know why. But I think I do. It's because the furniture doesn't fulfill a dream; it's purely an accessory, an accoutrement, to their otherwise-empty lives.

And what of all those vainglorious individuals who manipulate money and markets so they can amass riches on a far grander scale? They own for the sake of owning; acquire for the sake of acquiring. We watch with fascination as they go for it, grab the brass ring, seize the day—reach out and pluck whatever they want, seemingly without a qualm. We admire them, even as we condemn them, because they appear to possess a boldness we find absent in ourselves.

But there is an inherent problem in this approach, for what they seize is never enough, and so they always end up seizing more, until they discover to their astonishment that everything they thought they owned has sifted through their fingers like sand. But the boy who dreams of a blue sloop, who finally possesses it, who uses it and then passes it on to another after it has lost its utility for him—that boy possesses a blue sloop for all his days.

25

•

first
you
have
to
row
a
little
boat

FOUR

·

I LISTEN TO THE WIND
... AND THE WIND
TELLS ME WHAT TO DO

·

The wind came up out of the southwest at ten knots and surpassed fifteen on that day when I made my first test run. By the time I tacked out of the long canal, the bay was a seething mass of whitecaps from the mainland clear across to the barrier beach, eight miles away. A sailboat will not sail directly

27

into the wind; it will only sail at an acute angle to it, about forty-five degrees. But I wanted to hew as closely to it as possible as I headed due south for the fishing flats where I knew I would find the *Nimrod*.

Far off on the horizon, I saw the glistening water tower at Saltaire, a summer community on Fire Island. It loomed like a godsend, exactly the landmark I was looking for. I figured that if I aimed straight for it and held my course, regardless of the wind and waves, I would be sailing my sloop at precisely the proper angle for maximum efficiency. That's what happens when we lose our poise. Instead of paying closer heed to our immediate surroundings, we search for a fixed point way off in the distance in the vague hope that it will keep us from drowning.

I sat well up on the windward deck, opposite the sail, a counterweight against the force of the wind; each time the sloop heeled to leeward—the sail nearly touching the water—the tiller slipped out of my hand. As the boat righted herself naturally, I would seize the tiller with all my might, only to lose it when she heeled once more. I made my way across the bay, yawing like a drunkard, too scared to come off the windward deck, afraid that if I shifted my weight more toward the lee side of the boat I would capsize.

When I was about five miles off the mainland, I saw the stubby *Nimrod* anchored on the shoals with

29
•
first
you
have
to
row
a
little
boat

a fishing party aboard—and the captain waving at me furiously. I judged the tide was running high enough so that I could cross the sandbar without running aground. I sailed below *Nimrod's* stern, then headed up into the wind, leaving about ten feet between the two hulls. It seemed a safe distance, and it would have been more than enough if I had been sailing a lightweight duck blind or a wallowing hippopotamus. But every boat I had previously owned was a bobbing cork compared with this new mistress of mine.

She had eleven hundred pounds of leaded weight in her keel, and that gave her momentum, a condition of life about which I still had a lot to learn. The boat refused to stop; she kept plowing powerfully ahead even though I had pointed her up into the heavy wind and seas. At the last second I tried to veer off, but in my confusion I pushed the tiller the wrong way. My sharp-nosed bow rammed into *Nimrod's* gunwale, gouging out a hefty chunk of planking. The captain let out a low wail, but I knew he was vexed more by my sloppy tactics than the damage to his hull.

He disappeared into *Nimrod's* cabin, emerged with a saw in his hand, and stepped aboard my sloop. When he reached the cockpit, he promptly sawed my six-foot-long tiller in half without permission or ado.

"Too damn long," he said by way of explanation,

and then cast his hand over the roiling waters and added, "In this light breeze you want to sit down here on the lu'ard side."

He positioned himself on the lee side of the cockpit—the exact place I had been afraid to sit—and ordered me to cast off. He sat on the floorboards with the truncated tiller over his right shoulder, jutting past his ear. He didn't grab the stick for dear life, as I had, but held it lightly between his thumb and forefinger, as if he were listening to the sound of the water rising through the rudder post into the fingers of his hand. He was a musician playing an instrument that had been finely tuned.

"You've got to climb the wind," he said to me. "When you sail a boat, you've got to climb the wind all the time."

He told me that by sitting on the lee side, under the mainsail instead of on the deck opposite it, I could see the aft edge of the jib, the small sail in front of the mast. "Sail with the jib," he said. "Watch the jib way up high. Let the boat climb the wind until the jib luffs ever so gently near the peak, then ease off a hair until the flutter goes away. Then as the boat gains momentum, climb the wind some more."

Through the years I've encountered innumerable sailors who understood the theory of sailing and had no compunctions about explaining it to me—right down to its most technical point. The only trouble was that either they couldn't sail or, if they could, the sheer poetry of the boat in motion had passed beyond their ken. But it was from the captain's vivid imagery—Climb the wind!—that I first perceived the delicate balance between myself, my boat, and the sea.

The prevailing summer breeze on the Great South Bay blows out of the southwest with diurnal regularity, rising in the morning over the Atlantic, picking up speed throughout the day as the sun warms the land, and then falling off in the evening as the land gives up its heat. As a novice sailor I believed the summer wind was faithful, so steady I could set a course by it. What I had yet to learn was that the wind deceived me constantly about its direction and velocity, and that if I wanted to sail, and sail well, I had to abide by subtleties my senses could barely detect.

One moment the wind might blow slightly harder. When that happened, it would shift imperceptibly a compass point or two toward the west. The next moment it might wane. When that happened, it would shift a compass point or two toward the south. These shifts might elude me, but they didn't elude the sloop. With each puff she would climb higher into the fickle wind of her own volition, as if she had a knowing of her own.

What I had to do was stop steering with a vengeance and pay attention to what the sloop wanted to do. I had to hold the tiller gently between my thumb and forefinger, the way the captain showed

31

•

first
you
have
to
row
a
little
boat

me. I had to let the boat go, let her climb the wind until the peak of the foresail fluttered ever so slightly, and then I had to steer off the wind a fraction until the breeze filled the sail again and the fluttering disappeared. Then, as the wind picked up once more, I had to climb the wind, climb the wind— and let the elation of the surging sloop fill my soul.

To be at one with the wind is to be at home in the world, free of moral judgment. The sailor who refuses to abide by the wind sets his course by a mark on land, a water tower, a lighthouse, a church steeple. He holds rigidly to that mark, the way a king clings to his crown or a zealot to his certitude, immune to the currents swirling about his head. He doesn't sail the wind; he sails his dogmas, and his dogmas deaden his senses, stripping him of his ability to see, to think, to feel, to respond to his dilemma.

Such a sailor is a wastrel; he consumes more wind than he needs to get to where he wants to go, and so in the race to windward he is inevitably the last to cross the finish line. But that's the least of it, for of all the helmsmen I know he is the one with the least joy, because the light has gone out of him. In the end, all he has to show for his passage are his principles, and that is his tragedy.

He is the judge who is less interested in the victim than the letter of the law, the boss who is less interested in the well-being of his workers than his short-term-profit goals. What marks these people is their absolute rigidity. They refuse to adapt; they adhere religiously to their rules, their regulations, their schedules even as their Humpty-Dumpty world comes crashing down about their ears. We ask ourselves why they pursue their self-destructive ends so persistently, and the answer, at least in part, lies in the fact that they are like the sailor who never learned to climb the wind.

I come now, at this late juncture of my life, to this sudden realization: I have no destination, no real destination, in the literal sense. The destination, the place toward which my life is tending, is the journey itself and not the final stopping place. How I get there is more important than whether I arrive, although I will arrive, and what I must try to remember, now more than ever, is to listen to the wind, and the wind will tell me what to do.

33

•

first
you
have
to
row
a
little
boat

FIVE

·

WHO MADE
THIS BOAT?

·

*T*hought about this boat of
mine. Where did she come
from? Who created her?

I had acquired her from a
marine architect who had stripped her
decks and altered her rigging to his
liking, but that was renovation, not
genesis.

Someone owned her before he did,

and undoubtedly someone before that. The original purchaser, whoever he was, bought her from a shipyard in Greenport, way out on Long Island's North Fork, where all the Timber Points were built back in the 1920s. Mine was the third one to slide down the ways; I knew that because she bore the number 3 on her sails.

But she had progenitors, ships that sailed before her keel was laid, centuries before she was conceived, for she hadn't sprung forth full-blown with all her inbred wisdom, like Minerva from the head of Zeus.

I thought about my blue sloop's inherent virtues, which became more evident each time I sailed.

If I let go of the tiller, she headed straight up into the wind like a weather vane. Who taught her that?

When the wind filled the sails, it pushed the sloop sideways, yet she knifed ahead because she had a keel that translated lateral motion into forward thrust. How did it happen that she evolved this protruding backbone under her hull for steerage?

She had a stern rudder. There was a novel idea. What sage suddenly recognized the mechanical advantage of locating the steering mechanism in the rear?

When she floated at her mooring post, she immersed herself as far as her waterline. Who had calculated how deep a boat should sink, how high she should float, how much sea she should displace?

When she was under way and her sails were trimmed at exactly the correct angle to the wind,

she lay over "on her lines." When she tipped too
far, the wind spilled out of her canvas and she
popped back up rather than capsize. It was a comfort
to know that. But who figured out those critical
relationships among breeze, boat, and sail?

The designer? No, that didn't make sense. The
designer had undoubtedly learned the mathematics
at some university and applied it to the best of his
judgment when he computed the length, beam,
draft, and sail area of my Timber Point. But the idea
behind the mathematics—that preceded him. That
went back to antiquity.

Was there one genius, way back in the dim past,
who awakened one morning with the whole idea of
a sailing vessel worked out in his head? I began to
look into the history of sailing ships—the British,
the Spaniards, the Vikings, the Romans, the Greeks,
the Phoenicians, the Minoans, the Egyptians—to
see if I could locate him.

Of them all, the Phoenicians, who transformed
the Mediterranean Sea into their private trading lake,
intrigued me the most. They took the cedars of
Lebanon and converted them into wind-powered
cargo ships with broad, rectangular sails that plied
the seas from Tyre to Sidon to Carthage to Cadiz
and back again.

Ship begat ship: Northern European cogs, Italian
carracks, Spanish galleons, and Yankee clippers with
so many billowing sails that they looked as if they
might rise from the water and fly.

37
•
first
you
have
to
row
a
little
boat

Arabian dhows; Chinese junks; New Guinea *laka-tois*; Portuguese feluccas; Hawaiian canoes. Wherever there was sea and wind, there was a dipping sail.

In my own contained body of water, I saw catboats with one mast and one sail, sloops with one mast and two sails, and ketches, yawls, and schooners with two masts and three sails.

What did a mariner desire? Stability? Speed to windward? A boat that ran well before the wind? Did he want to race? Cruise? Sail an ocean, a river, a lake, a bay? Whatever his ambition, there was a boat for him.

But I couldn't discover the one individual who first got the idea of putting a sail on a boat to capture the wind. And then a notion occurred to me, a topsy-turvy truth for a boy who had been taught to believe all things had a precise beginning in place and time. I couldn't find out who first conceived of a sailing vessel, for the obvious reason that there was no such person. The wind-borne boat originated in the minds of many men, probably in different places at about the same time, and like a living organism it adapted to its surroundings as it evolved.

In school I had been told the stories of the great American inventors: Fulton and his steamboat, Marconi and his wireless, Edison and his light bulb, Bell and his telephone, Whitney and his cotton gin. Each of these individuals, according to legend, had disappeared into his lonely attic and emerged with a miraculous device that changed the world.

These were inspiring myths concocted to instill in students a pride in what teachers liked to call "good old-fashioned Yankee ingenuity." But my exploration into the origins of the sailing ship convinced me these tales were totally implausible. The technologies credited to these men couldn't possibly have materialized out of nowhere—anymore than my sailboat could have floated down out of the sky.

Products, like people, have their lineage and if we take the pains, we can trace their family tree. Edison, Fulton, Bell, and all the others had silent partners— the tinkers, mechanics, engineers, and scientists of the past—to whom they owed an incalculable debt, whether they wanted to admit it or not.

My high school history book told me that Orville and Wilbur Wright went down to Kitty Hawk one December day in 1903 and made the world's first flight in a gas-powered, heavier-than-air machine. Just like that. A plane is a ship in air, but this text had serious transgressions, for it omitted the magic.

What about Icarus, who flew so close to the sun that his wax wings melted?

What about Archytas, the Greek scholar who built a wooden pigeon that flew through the air?

What about Leonardo da Vinci's remarkable sixteenth-century sketches of a flying machine with flapping wings?

39
•
first
you
have
to
row
a
little
boat

What about the Marquis d'Arlandes and Jean F. Pilâtre de Rozier, who flew over Paris in a linen balloon?

What about Sir George Cayley, who lay down the early ground rules for a fixed-wing plane powered by propellers?

What about Otto Lilienthal of Germany, who built gossamer gliders and flew them for hundreds of feet?

And what about the American, Samuel P. Langley, who built a steam-powered model called an aerodrome?

Each individual, each event predated Kitty Hawk, and each led inexorably, through a conscious, striving force, an élan vital, toward that fateful day on the Cape Hatteras sand dunes.

In our vain attempt to eulogize our patron inventors, we forget that human knowledge is cumulative, a cooperative endeavor. We stand on the shoulders of giants: Archimedes, Galileo, Newton, Darwin, Einstein, to name a few. But for each individual of stature, there are untold others who, for better or worse, helped piece together our civilization—and whose names we will never know.

Nor was this sloop of mine purely an engineer's conceit. She was born of song and sculpture, too. I could hear it in the hum of her rigging; I could see it in the flare of her hull. She owed a debt to the epics of Homer and the fugues of Bach. She was an eloquent fusion of the war within ourselves, the war which tears us apart, the ceaseless conflict between science and art.

We can't separate what we believe from who we are. I have friends who hold up literature as the highest expression of human yearning, and being a writer myself I find this poetical view of existence hard to resist. But in my rare moments of objectivity, I realize this is chauvinism of the worst kind. I can't deplore the geometry of Euclid and praise the plays of Shakespeare, as if one were barbarous and the other divine.

Nor can I claim the scientific world poses a greater threat to human survival than the artistic one. For the truth is that art runs amok as readily as science. How can we separate the propaganda machine of Goebbels from the ovens at Buchenwald? And yet, there are occasions when the passion of the artist is more powerful than the armaments of the tyrant. If this wasn't so, a formerly imprisoned playwright wouldn't have become president of Czechoslovakia.

Are these the conflicting worlds of C. P. Snow—art versus science, science versus art—all over again? I don't think so; I don't believe the two exist as discreet entities. The fact that we try to split them apart is a symptom of an all-too-human malaise that causes us to stake out our turf and erect artificial boundaries instead of tearing them down. Artist and scientist are mythmakers alike, playing off one another's dreams—although it is sometimes difficult to convince a partisan that this is so.

•

first
you
have
to
row
a
little
boat

I know a research scientist for a large corporation who is as dogmatic as an educated man can be. He denigrates painting, literature, music at every opportunity, saying he has never seen a work of art that can compare with the elegance of a binomial equation. When I told him once that I believed all living creatures had a soul, this man of inquiry, of pure reason, snorted as he walked away. He didn't ask me what I meant by a soul, how I defined it. He didn't care to know.

Of course, I know artists who are just as blind, who hold the mechanical mind in contempt, as if it were capable of producing nothing but bombs. I am suspicious of technology myself; I didn't buy an electric typewriter until computers came on the market, and I didn't buy a computer until my editors insisted that I submit discs instead of typewritten pages. I am not proud of this tendency of mine to be dragged protesting into the future, as if I could through my private boycott call a halt to the electronic age.

I bought my computer, and I since have come to a better understanding of where to invest my energies. I can no more than King Canute hold up my hand and stem the tide. Just as ship begat ship, so tool begat tool. The day we invented the screw and plow, we also invented the computer and plane; it was only a matter of time, because it was sealed in the genes.

These thoughts which occur to me with such

43

•

first
you
have
to
row
a
little
boat

intensity now began to gather, unspoken and unformulated, when I was still a boy, skimming alone with the wind, the tiller in my hand. Why that was so, I can't say. It may be that I was, through my sloop, searching for some lost aspect of myself. And since my parents were dead, I had no impediment in the present to obstruct my view of the past. When I sailed my boat, when she surged in the wind, I felt a mystical bond with those unnamed artisans who were my forebears.

I was the beneficiary of their collective genius. This boat, an amalgam of mechanics and music, was the highest gift within their power to pass down the ages to me. When I knew that, I also knew the truth about creation. Many lives, going back thousands of years, had gone into the making of my sloop, just as many lives, going back into time unknown, had gone into the making of me.

SIX

·

THE SHORTEST
DISTANCE BETWEEN
TWO POINTS IS
A ZIGZAG LINE

·

I invited a black-haired siren named Martha Coogan to sail with me. I was attracted to her, as was every other boy in my class, but I had an advantage over them. I had a beautiful blue sloop as lure.

I was studying plane geometry at the time, and I was mindful of Euclid's first

45

and most important postulate: The shortest distance between two points is a straight line. When I invited Martha aboard my boat, my intentions may not have been honorable, but I was certain I had chosen the quickest, most direct route to reach my goal.

Martha accepted right away. What I didn't realize was that she was more interested in being seen on my boat than being seen with me. She positioned herself conspicuously on the bow and posed in her bathing suit, but as soon as a wave sprayed over the deck she retreated to the cockpit. Martha Coogan didn't like to get wet.

I decided I would head for Saltaire, dock the sloop, and walk across the barrier beach to the ocean where we could swim in the surf. But that Fire Island community was directly into the wind, so I had to sail a zigzag, tacking course to get there. That bothered Martha even more than the salt spray messing her carefully composed hair.

"Won't this boat go any faster?" she demanded to know. "And why are you going off in this crazy direction? Can't you see Saltaire is over there?"

I almost made the fatal mistake of trying to explain why I couldn't sail faster, why I had to tack. But there are moments when we sense that explanations are futile, and this was one of them. I snapped back, "I tell you what, Martha. Why don't you find yourself a guy who owns a speedboat. Then you can buzz around the bay any old way you please." With that, I sailed back to shore and dumped her on dry land.

47

•

first
you
have
to
row
a
little
boat

Euclid was wrong. The shortest distance between two points wasn't a straight line . . . at least not when it came to sailing a boat or wooing a girl.

The next time I saw Martha Coogan, she was with another boy aboard a skiff driven by a pair of high-powered outboard motors. They were rioting around the bay, searching for themselves. They circled me several times—Martha even waved in her imperious way as they sped by—and then headed straight for Fire Island, where I, with no small degree of envy, envisioned them swimming together in the surf.

But no! About halfway across the bay, they turned around and headed back. They passed me again, going full blast in the opposite direction, while I was still on the same tack. I may have been traveling slantwise and at a slower pace, but I knew where I was going, which is a lot more than I could say for them.

The skiff's rear end plowed deeply into the water, raising a huge wake, and its bottom pounded with enough force to jolt the teeth out of their jaws, but they threw their heads back in laughter, as if they were having the greatest time, and maybe they were. They didn't have to pay the slightest heed to elements that ruled simple folk like me who preferred to sail. They had a mighty gasoline engine and above its roar they couldn't possibly have heard the whistle of the wind.

I was annoyed, of course, but with the passage of years I respond to such behavior less with irritation than with resignation and regret. I am truly sorry for individuals who feel they must harness themselves to an artificial source of power and then tool about aimlessly, pretending they're enjoying themselves; and I am even sorrier for a society that supplies the motive·force that makes such misdirection possible. They mistake motion for accomplishment, as if they think they can defy their destiny if they move fast enough.

"Go round about, Peer Gynt, go round about!" The legendary hero of Henrik Ibsen's poetical drama tries to flail the Boyg, the invisible black force of Norse folklore, when he encounters it deep in the woods, speaking to him, blocking his way. The first time I heard those words spoken from a stage, I felt them echoing in my heart and I knew what the mysterious voice coming from nowhere, coming from everywhere, was trying to say. "Don't go straight up against the god of the wind, Peer Gynt, because you can't prevail. But don't lose sight of your destination, either, for the quest of your life is to discover who you are."

Poor egotistical Peer Gynt is too self-absorbed to understand. He sets forth, tramping purposelessly about the world, ignoring the warning from the Boyg.

He squanders a lifetime in wild adventuring, fleeing from his fate, avoiding the issues of his life, returning only in the moment before death to home, wife, steadfast love, where he finds at last his true self.

To tack a boat, to sail a zigzag course, is not to deny our destination or our destiny—despite how it may appear to those who never dare to take the tiller in their hand. Just the opposite: It's to recognize the obstacles that stand between ourselves and where we want to go, and then to maneuver with patience and fortitude, making the most of each leg of our journey, until we reach our landfall.

The games we play, the games that command our everyday attention, do so for reasons we often fail to see. Baseball and football are our national fictions for the simple reason that they're accurate representations of truth about the life we live. A runner on second must advance to third before he can score, even though the fastest way home is a diagonal through the heart of the diamond over the pitcher's mound. The most direct route from the line of scrimmage to the end zone is straight ahead, but it's a rare touchdown that's made that way; there are too many would-be tacklers between the ball carrier and the goal.

Above all else, the nature of our existence demands that we master reality. I wanted to be a freelance writer as far back as I can remember. To be a writer was to be myself; I understood that instinct-

49
•
first
you
have
to
row
a
little
boat

ively. My father was a free-lance artist, and I'm sure the model of independence he set for me as he worked at his easel was indelibly imprinted on my brain long before he died. I wanted to create and sell what I created, just as he had, for that was the true measure of my self-worth.

But I had many a zig and zag before I published a magazine article or sold a book. I married and fathered children while I was still a young man; that was a deeply rooted drive that had to be satisfied. I had to replace the family that had been; I had to become the father I had lost. Once I had children, I was obliged to support them and that forced me to keep a job with a regular paycheck, since free-lance writing was (and still is) a precarious livelihood at best.

I worked as a newspaperman and magazine editor, an important initial tack because it taught me my craft. I worked next as the editorial director of a public relations firm in Manhattan, another important tack because it gave me contacts and showed me the way "the real world" (as my colleagues liked to put it) worked. I left public relations to earn a graduate degree at a university, yet another critical tack because it was while I was studying that I began to write and sell what I wrote.

The skills I acquired as a sailor served me well, for they gave me a sense of pace which I might not otherwise possess. I see people all about me who have never developed an adequate inner clock and who are never at one with the wind because of it. The frantic individual tacks too soon, jumping from job to job, friendship to friendship, spouse to spouse, losing headway at every turn. The obtuse individual remains on the same tack too long, investing too much time, talent, and energy in a course that takes him far from his avowed objective. But the seasoned sailor stays on the same tack as long as it appears advantageous, and then, at the appropriate moment, pushes the tiller toward the sail and deftly changes direction.

Each separate tack calls for a major readjustment. The bow moves across the face of the wind. The sail swings from one side of the sloop to the other. Helmsman and mate shift position. The land looms from a different quarter. But if the maneuver is handled fluently, the boat continues to surge ahead with a minimum loss of momentum.

In due course we arrive, if it can be said that we ever fully arrive. The truth is that there are destinations beyond destinations, and so the confirmed sailor goes on tacking forever.

51

·

first
you
have
to
row
a
little
boat

SEVEN

·

"IN IRONS"

·

*W*hat is liberty? We say of a boat skimming the water with light foot, "How
free she runs," when we mean, how
perfectly she is adjusted to the force of
the wind, how perfectly she obeys the great breath out
of the heavens that fills her sails. Throw her head into
the wind and see how she will halt and stagger, how
every sheet will shiver and her whole frame be shaken,
how instantly she is "in irons," in the expressive phrase
of the sea. She is free only when you have let her fall
off again and have recovered once more her nice adjustment to the forces she must obey and cannot defy.

WOODROW WILSON
Twenty-eighth President of the United States

53

I knew the wisdom of Wilson's words long before I found them on a calendar filled with notable quotations sent to me by my local hardware store. Yet I was more indebted to the proprietor than he knew, for his gift reminded me of the terrible panic that overtook me the first time I was shackled by the wind. I had boarded my sloop, raised her sails, and cast off from my mooring post, confident—in my innocence—that I would have no trouble reaching open water, where the breeze was fair.

The bulkheaded canal in which I docked my sloop was nearly a mile long, arrow-straight and narrow— no wider than fifty yards. When the wind was from the south, as it was that summer day, it blew directly up its north-south axis, and I had to tack more than half its length to reach the bay. It was a tricky operation; I would barely gain headway on one tack when I would be forced to come about on the opposite tack to avoid crashing into the bulkhead, or a vessel tied up at a mooring post, or one of a series of overlapping piers that jutted out at right angles from the land.

As if that wasn't enough, the wind itself, which blew steadily in the bay, was untrustworthy in the canal. It got trapped behind the broad Victorian homes that lined the shore; sometimes it swept around their front porches in unexpected directions and other times it blew in their back doors, never to emerge. As a result, the canal was a veritable obstacle course, filled with dead spots, fluky winds and immovable barriers, a test of skill for the experienced sailor and a potential disaster-in-waiting for a tyro like me.

I began to crisscross the canal, each zig, each zag bringing me closer to the bay. I had but one thought: to make as much forward progress as possible on each tack. What I didn't know during those early days when my sloop and I were getting to know each other was that if I wanted to retain control I had to keep her moving, moving at all costs—to heed the dictates of the shifting wind. It was, in fact, far better to sail back up the canal, away from the bay, in the direction from which I had come, than to lose headway.

In sailing, as in life, momentum is a valued commodity, the secondary source of power that keeps us going long after the original source has disappeared. In sports, we tend to favor those athletes who are on a winning streak. "The momentum is with them," we like to say—by which we mean that they appear to have transcended their own inherent abilities and are surging ahead on the accumulated power of the past. But we tend to forget that the reverse is also true. If winners tend to keep on winning, then losers tend to keep on losing, for the physical principle governing inertia is a two-edged sword. It states that a body in motion tends to stay in motion—and a body at rest tends to stay at rest.

A sailboat depends upon a bellyful of wind in her sails to keep her hull thrusting through the sea. But

55
•
first
you
have
to
row
a
little
boat

as we bring her about, as her bow crosses the breeze, she passes through a danger zone. "Throw her head into the wind," Wilson says, "and see how she will halt and stagger, how every sheet will shiver and her whole frame be shaken. . . ." The sails lose their wind; they flatten and flap noisily. But if the boat has sufficient momentum, she will continue to turn until the wind bellies out the sail again on the other side.

When that happens, we experience the wondrous thrill, the exultation that comes with the sudden return of personal liberty. The boat heels and takes off with the breeze, and the helmsman—if not aloud, then in his soul—lets out a cry of sheer joy, for he knows he has recaptured control of his life and destiny. But if we dissipate our momentum, if we try to come about without sufficient accumulated force, we lose the element as essential to our being as air itself; we lose our freedom to act as we choose. That's what happened to me as I sailed my zigzag course toward the bay.

Halfway out of the canal, I miscalculated badly. The wind, funneling between two houses, momentarily shifted ninety degrees. Instead of adjusting, I continued to cut across the waterway on the same angle, still trying to make as much forward progress as possible, not noting that my sails, devoid of wind, were luffing and my boat staggering to a standstill. I sailed as close to the bulkhead as I dared and then, pushing the tiller toward the mainsail, tried to come about and head for the opposite shore. But I lacked enough momentum to carry the bow across the face of the wind and, "in the expressive phrase of the sea," I was instantly "in irons."

I couldn't tell if the boat was inching forward, slipping sideways, or drifting backward—when she was undoubtedly doing all three. I jiggled the tiller desperately, but she wouldn't respond to the action of the rudder, for a boat without wind in her sails is a boat out of control, subject only to the buffeting action of the breeze. Boxed in, she blows about, catching a snippet of wind here, a fragment there, losing it long before it can billow out the sail and give the helmsman the forward motion he needs to steer.

I was completely helpless and there was nothing I could do as the hull of my beautiful blue sloop banged against a mooring post and the sail caught on a wooden cross arm, which threatened to puncture a hole in the canvas. An amused crowd of would-be sailors gathered at the end of a nearby pier and began to offer unsolicited advice.

"Backwind the jib!" one shouted.

"Push the tiller the other way!" another instructed.

"Drop the sails!" a third called out.

I clambered out on the bow and, using the mooring post as a fulcrum, slowly swung the boat around so that the sails could catch the wind, and then pushed off as hard as I could. It wasn't the most elegant maneuver, but it worked. Back in the

57
•
first
you
have
to
row
a
little
boat

cockpit, I trimmed the sheets and in a moment had her obeying "the great breath out of the heavens" that filled her sails once more. I switched back and forth across the canal, taking care never to lose headway, and in a few minutes I was sailing freely in the spanking breeze that swept across the bay.

"Each tack is a transition," the captain had said to me during one of my earlier sailing lessons, as if he knew I would find myself "in irons" one fine day. "Each time you come about," he added, "there's a frightening moment as you pass through the eye of the wind." I had dismissed his warning, partly out of ignorance, partly out of arrogance, but now I had discovered the meaning of his words from the greatest teacher of all: experience. To change directions is a difficult tactic at best, and we're doomed to failure, destined to become a prisoner of the wind, if we attempt it in an ineffectual way.

There's only one sure way to come about, and that is to gather momentum on the course we're on. As a youth, I applied that lesson narrowly to the handling of my sloop, but with the passage of time I saw that it was a verity, as true for life on land as for life at sea. I might abhor the tack I was on—and I recall two memorable occasions when I did. Early in life, I deplored the college I was attending; later, I despised the job I held. But I had to stay with each long enough to gather wherewithal (decent grades in the first case, sufficient savings in the second) to carry myself through the eye of the wind. If I quit one or the other prematurely, I would founder and the wind would take over my life, blowing me in directions I had no desire to go.

59
•
first
you
have
to
row
a
little
boat

I know a talented young man who majored in music in college, only to find when he earned his degree that he didn't want a career in that field. Wisely, he didn't attempt to come about at once. He worked for two years, playing his saxophone in a dance band aboard a cruise ship, stashing away his money while he tried to figure out what he really wanted to do. Eventually, he decided to study law, and by then he had earned enough to put himself through graduate school. Although he wasn't a sailor, he thought like one; he understood that at all costs he had to avoid being trapped trying to sail dead into the wind.

I know another young man who casts constantly about, hopping from one job to another. He says he's trying to figure out where he fits in, what he wants to do with his life, and I sympathize with that goal in its entirety. But I notice he never really gives himself a chance; the jobs he takes aren't the ones he selects; they're the ones he's forced to take because his rent is due, and so he's "in irons" all the time.

What's at stake is nothing less than personal autonomy—our capacity to empower ourselves so that we may choose the course of our life rather than have it chosen for us by others whose values may differ radically from our own. We may make a decision to go our own way, which is the only true way, but if we're caught without wind in our sails we'll find ourselves captive, doing the bidding of those we detest. And the tragedy is this: We may never give the gift which is ourselves to those we love or find out who we truly are.

EIGHT

·

GOING

WITH THE WIND

·

*E*arly one morning when the wind was light, I raised my sails and tacked toward Fire Island. With each passing moment the southwesterly grew stronger; by midday I knew it would be kicking up whitecaps across the bay. But in the gentle grip of those first wafts blowing landward from the Atlantic, I soared like a seabird on the thermals of a summer day.

When I reached the barrier beach, I waded ashore, walked across the narrow spit of sand to the ocean, where I swam in the surf, basked in the sun, dozed on the sloping breast of a dune. Late in the day, when the sun was falling in the western sky, I returned to my anchored sloop, hoisted her sails, and headed home with the breeze behind.

I sat high on the windward deck, watching the pursuing swells as they rolled under the hull, lifting and lowering the boat, rocking it like a cradle. Since sloop and I were moving at almost the same speed as the wind, I could barely feel its refreshing touch against my face. The warm sun beat down on my back. I slumped on the cockpit floorboards and closed my eyes, telling myself that if there ever was a time when I could sink into blissful indolence, it was on this long run home.

The fact that I was sitting so low obstructed my view, but it also saved my life. In an instant, without warning, the wind slipped behind my outstretched mainsail, picked up the heavy wooden boom and threw it with tremendous force clear across the boat. It crashed into a stainless steel stay, ripping the fastening out of the deck and tipping the mast. Had my torso been in a position to intercept the action, my head surely would have been knocked from my neck.

Perhaps the wind had shifted slightly. Perhaps a

63
·
first
you
have
to
row
a
little
boat

wave had tipped the sloop too far toward the north-east. Perhaps, through inattention, I had steered the boat too far off the wind. Whatever the reason, I had committed the one maneuver a sailor dreads the most: the accidental jibe.

When he tacks, the bow crosses the wind; there is a momentary dead spot and he needs momentum to keep the hull moving when the sails are flat. But when he jibes, the stern crosses the wind; there is no dead spot, no warning at all. He doesn't need to miscalculate by much—a mere fraction in the wrong direction and the wind will gather behind the sail and shoot it across the deck with killing force.

There is a proper way to turn when going with the wind—and an accomplished sailor knows exactly how to do it. First, he trims in the sail as closely as possible so that it doesn't have so far to swing, and then he lets the mainsheet run out quickly on the other side as the boom sweeps across the deck. Even so, there are times, especially in a heavy wind, when even the most experienced sailor will elect to go roundabout—to make a 350-degree turn and bring his bow across the wind rather than a 10-degree turn and jibe.

The danger in jibing, as in most things, results not from deliberation but inadvertence, not from caution but heedlessness. I had ample time to reflect on that while my deck was being patched, my mast properly stepped, and my stay bolted back in place. The captain, seeing my sloop in the shipyard, called

to me across the narrow waterway from the bow of
the *Nimrod*.

"What happened?"

"I jibed—when I didn't mean to."

"Ahh," he said, "running with the wind—it seems
so easy. The breeze fills the sail and blows you right
along. You turn your head for a second to watch the
wake. The next thing you know, the boom
comes. . . ."

"I know," I said, "I know."

But, in truth, I didn't know, for I was to jibe many
times in my life before I understood that going with
the wind is the most dangerous course of all. Like
so many others, I found it deceptively easy to let
myself be lulled into that false sense of security that
so often surrounds us when we're in the sway of a
following breeze. Once I understood that I was least
safe when I was half awake, I roused myself from
my lethargy and took my life into my own hands.

One of my first acts was to quit a job I disliked,
which I was clinging to mainly for the benefits, and
enter the ranks of the self-employed—to be what I
had always wanted to be even though it meant I
would have to provide my own health insurance
and retirement fund. I had no sooner submitted
my resignation when the president of the company
summoned me to his office and accused me of com-
mitting the sin of self-pride.

"You're jeopardizing the future of your family,"

65
•
first
you
have
to
row
a
little
boat

he said. "And what for? So you can pursue your personal whim. How can you do that to them!"

I wanted to tell him the parable of the accidental jibe, but I refrained.

Years later, when it was apparent that I hadn't made a wrong move, a casual acquaintance, a career executive for a large corporation, approached me at a dinner party and asked, "You're a free-lance writer, aren't you?"

"That's right," I said.

"Isn't that a dicey game?"

In a sense, he was right. The nature of my occupation dictated that I live by my wits without the guarantee of a regular paycheck. "I suppose it is," I said. "The truth is that I don't know right this moment how much money I'll make next month."

"I don't think I could live like that," he said. "It's too precarious for me." He sucked in his cheeks, I'm sure secretly congratulating himself on the stability of his position compared with mine.

A few months later, I ran into the same man again and found out he had lost his job. Faced with stiff competition from abroad, his company had made wholesale layoffs in its labor force. He was stunned by his employer's unexpected action, and I distinctly remember his words: "I was a good worker. I was a loyal employee. I never dreamed my company would do this to me. I guess I was naïve."

Naïve? Perhaps. Or maybe, like me, he had to

learn about complacency—about putting too much faith in a following wind.

Of all the calamities that can overwhelm a life, there is none more final than sudden death. I know a woman who existed for twenty-five years within the confines of a loving marriage in which her husband tended to her every need. She never had to trouble herself with such mundane things as writing a check or repairing a car. She sailed peaceably along in the warmth of his abiding breeze. Then, in his mid-forties, he was struck down by a heart attack— and all the stays, all the supports, all the running rigging of her life were swept away. To her credit, she eventually overcame her fears and taught herself what she needed to know, but she was a long time recovering from that unexpected jibe.

What happened to that woman happens to most of us at some point during our lives. We leave our harbor home with a fair wind behind and we let it push us mindlessly along. The vessel planes through the sea; the shoreline disappears. We aren't using the wind; the wind is using us, blowing us willy-nilly in its own direction.

Miles out, catastrophe strikes and we find we must sail our disabled ship back to port with its mast tipped or its sail torn. But now the wind is no longer at our back; it's in our face, and we are forced by the circumstances we created through our own thoughtlessness to beat against it in order to get back to the place where we began.

67

•

first
you
have
to
row
a
little
boat

I learned this lesson—which seems so obvious but which is rarely observed—early in my sailing life. It's better by far, if we have the choice, to sail into the wind when we leave port and then, at the end of our journey, to fly home with the breeze behind.

Shortly after my initial mishap, I jibed again— and then again. I seemed to have a talent for it. I brought my problem to the captain and he boarded my boat, carrying a long, sturdy pole, which he stowed below the deck. He sailed downwind with me, and it was under his tutelage that I discovered why I lost control of my sloop and let the wind slip behind the sail. Most sailing vessels have what's called a weather helm—a natural tendency to turn into the wind. Each time my sloop headed upwind of its own volition, I compensated by steering downwind, but every now and then I overcompensated, causing an accidental jibe.

When I had finally mastered the fine art of going with the wind, the captain said, "What you need is a whisker pole."

"A whisker pole?"

I had never heard of such a thing. But he had come prepared. He removed the pole from under the deck and took it up to the bow, where he fixed one end to the mast, the other to the jib. He returned to the helm and sailed so that my mainsail hung way out on one side of the boat and my jib, steadied by the whisker pole, way out on the other.

We were going "wing and wing"—and what an apt sea term that is! Both sails, mainsail and jib, are spread like the wings of a soaring bird so they can best capture the following breeze. When I took the tiller, I could feel the surge, as if the billowing sails were pulling the sloop clear out of the sea and into the air.

Above my desk I keep a reproduction of a painting by Georgia O'Keeffe titled *Brown Sail, Wing and Wing, Nassau.* I suspect O'Keeffe was sitting where the helmsman sits, where I so often sat, when the vision for this evocative oil on canvas came to her. Although it's set in the Bahamas, I feel, whenever I glance up at it, as if I'm aboard this sloop, sailing the Great South Bay.

I see the world as O'Keeffe saw it—mainsail set out to starboard, jib to port. Above the sails puffy clouds blow across a summer sky; under the boom a lighthouse looms on a point of land against a pale blue sea. It all appears so peaceful, so tranquil, but I know it's a delusion, that the whole being of the unseen helmsman is engaged in a delicate balancing act. Veer too far one way and the jib will lose its wind; veer too far the other way and the mainsail will crash across the deck.

But it's not puffy clouds or pale sea that pulls me into this painting; it's the color of the sails. I've seen white sails, red sails, blue sails—sails of almost every hue except the one the painter chose. I have to believe that O'Keeffe, with her artist's instinct, fully

69

•

first
you
have
to
row
a
little
boat

grasped the threatening aspect of this downwind course, and that is why she painted the broad wing-spread of the sails, like a harrier in flight, a dark and ominous brown.

The painting, perched as it is above my desk, is a constant reminder that I live in perilous times. Even in my most secure moments, when I lie in bed with loving arms about me, I know that this is so. I try to persuade myself that I'm safer than my Stone Age ancestors because my world has a civilized veneer, but the truth is that I'm no more protected in my clapboard house than they were in their cave.

The voice of an ancient forebear rises within me and issues a warning cry. The cougar still lurks on the ledge over my head; the barbarian horde still threatens my town. I put my trust in the electronic appliances of my age; surely they will defend me against the pestilence that rises without warning and spreads like locusts across the land. But once again I know I am allowing myself to be deceived. The only security I know, that I will ever know, lies in me. And so I sit high on the windward deck and tell myself to watch the sail, watch the wind, and beware the jibe.

N I N E

·

BECALMED

·

Day after day, day after day
We stuck, nor breath nor motion;
As idle as a painted ship
Upon a painted ocean.

SAMUEL TAYLOR COLERIDGE
The Rime of the Ancient Mariner

*D*uring those early days when my blue sloop and I were first getting to know each other, I found the wind was an ever-present friend and I came to count on it. I beat into it, ran with it, or sailed sideways to it on a broad reach, confident that it would always be there, that it would never let me down.

It is perhaps an all-too-human frailty to suppose that a favorable wind will blow forever—that it will never die. But I indulged myself in that deception, for the truth is that while the breeze was in my face or on my back I found it impossible to imagine what it would be like to be caught in a dead calm. I knew that the wind might stop—I had heard of such a thing. But I regarded it as one of those unlucky conditions of life, like disease and death, that happen to others, not to me.

But one early fall day I discovered I wasn't immune to the moods of the sea. I tacked out of the long canal in a brisk southwesterly breeze, and all through a long, soaking afternoon I plowed through the whitecaps, my lee deck awash. I trimmed my sheets as far as I dared; the boat heeled, the mainsail nearly touched the water, and for an instant I thought I might capsize. I headed up into the wind, averting disaster, and then I repeated the maneuver—not once but many times. I knew I was tempting fate with my brinkmanship, but I was drawn by the danger and too exhilarated to stop.

It was late in the day when I headed home; the autumn sun was dipping below the horizon and the land was rapidly relinquishing its heat. When I was about a mile from shore, earth and sea, as though in conspiracy, reached a state of equilibrium—they were both the same temperature. I had never known the breeze to die completely; usually there was a trace to push the boat along, but at that moment the trusted thermals disappeared. My sails went limp, the bay went flat, and "we stuck, nor breath nor motion."

Only a short time before, my blue sloop and I had been dipping in the wind, darting through the waves, the salt spray flying over the bow and dousing my hair. I had no destination; I was simply sailing to and fro, halfway between the barrier beach and the mainland, taking the fresh breath out of the ocean for granted. And now the vagrant wind had vanished without the slightest hint of where it had gone.

I wasn't in imminent danger. My boat was drifting placidly on even keel, and I could plainly see the blinking lights of land in the gathering dusk. Even so, a tremor of fear swept over me, a chill dread that so often rises from within when we lose the motive power that drives us on. I had become addicted to motion, as if the sheer movement of the sloop gave meaning to my life, and now I was forced to face alone the frightening stillness of the sea.

"I have to do something; I have to do something!" I kept saying to myself.

In desperation, I seized the tiller and tried to propel the boat forward by jiggling it forcibly, a tactic that resulted in considerable commotion and precious little headway. I pushed the sail to starboard and then to port, hoping it might puff out magically,

73

•

first
you
have
to
row
a
little
boat

but there was no ripple on the water, no stir in the air. At that moment I would have gladly traded the calm that surrounded me for a gale. "Blow! Please blow!" I pleaded. But I was powerless, absolutely powerless; there was nothing I could do.

After a while I stretched flat on my back on the deck, with my hands under my head, and looked beyond the sails, beyond the spars, into the deepening sky. I watched the rim of the earth rise and envelop the sun, and the moon hang its crescent beside the evening star. I watched the beacon from the Fire Island Light, six times each minute, swing across the darkening bay. I saw the dome of heaven turn from purple to black, and I was startled when a night heron from nowhere perched atop my mast.

I had seen herons before, standing motionless in the shallows, waiting for their prey, their moment to strike, and I had seen them roosting in the willows along the shore, but I had never seen one alight on a mast. Looking upward from the deck, I couldn't see his black crown, but I knew from his hunched posture exactly who he was. Observant and serene, he gazed into the sea, peering below the surface calm, as if he was searching for a change of tide, a shift of wind, a favorable sign.

I sat upright and stared at that strange and stately bird, wishing I could ask him what he was looking for and how he could sit so quietly and composed for so long. He possessed the secret of stillness, a quality that was foreign to me, and I wondered if he was born with it—if it was locked in the sinews of his slender legs and the unruffled feathers of his wings—or if he had learned it as an imperative of survival in a world he couldn't control.

Could he read the future below the surface of the tranquil sea? I doubted it. I believed that like me he was waiting for the future to reveal itself in the present, the fleeting present, and then with innate wisdom he would fly off to a distant shore and fish the shoals.

I developed a grudging admiration for the bird, for his silent powers of perception, for his uncanny patience and capacity for solitude. It was as if he knew that before he could leave his perch he would have to pass through this desperate calm. As I observed him, my dread dissolved and in its place arose an awareness of my surroundings, of myself, that was far more acute than when I was plunging mindlessly through the waves.

I realized I didn't have to do something; I had to do nothing—that was the unalterable condition imposed upon me by the god of the winds. I had to remain as unhurried as the heron and wait for the breeze to return, as I knew it would, although I knew no better than the bird when it would blow or from what quadrant of the compass.

I gazed across the water, looking for telltale ripples; and although I couldn't foresee the coming of the wind, I could try to figure out what it was up to. In the past I had witnessed the southwesterly shift

75
•
first
you
have
to
row
a
little
boat

a compass point or two to the west as it picked up speed—or switch slightly to the south as it waned. But this breeze hadn't shifted; it had disappeared, as if it had been sucked up through a hole in the sky.

A boy in an outboard launch zipped by. Seeing that I was drifting idly, he cut his engine and called, "Want a tow?"

I carried no auxiliary power, and the idea of being towed into port behind a noxious kicker offended me. Even so, if he had made his offer a half hour earlier I might've accepted, but now I found it disquieting. I had tacked out of the harbor that morning in a stiff breeze; I had sailed that breeze through the long afternoon. On the way home, that breeze had died—and now I was awaiting the mystery of its reappearance so I could complete the natural cycle of my day. I answered without hesitation, "No thanks. I'm waiting for the wind."

An hour later I felt a puff from the north. The sails luffed ever so lightly; I quickly trimmed the sheets and a wisp of wind nudged the boat along. I looked up at the tip of my mast and the night heron was gone.

The wind had done a complete about-face, turned 180 degrees. I felt ridiculous for not knowing beforehand what now seemed so obvious. The wind could shift an imperceptible compass point or two without pausing, but it couldn't make a radical change—it couldn't go from southwest to northeast—without first passing through a period of calm.

77
•
first
you
have
to
row
a
little
boat

I aimed for a light at the head of the harbor and I was soon skimming up the canal toward my berth. When I arrived, my guardian uncle was there, standing nervously beside his car, his headlights pointing at the mooring post, as if to show the way.

"Were you worried?" I asked.

"I was for a while. But then I called the captain. He told me you probably lost the wind but not to worry because sooner or later you would find it again."

I forgot about the night heron, or, to be more precise, I stored him in a remote recess of my brain, for I don't think we ever give up the powerful images that transfigure our lives. They lie dormant, crouching in darkness, waiting for the right moment to arise—provided we don't push them so far into the depths of ourselves that they suffocate and die.

Two decades later he surfaced again when I was engaged in a mighty wrestling match with myself. I was pursuing my career, pressing toward an ephemeral vision of commercial success, not knowing what I wanted or where I was going and too caught up in the tumult of the quest to stop and figure it out. And then one day without warning, while dodging traffic on my way to work in midtown Manhattan, I dropped like a wounded animal with a spasm in the hollow of my thigh.

The pain persisted; the spasms occurred more frequently. When I reached the point where I needed crutches to walk, my surgeon decided he had no choice except to fuse the bones in my hip. He understood the osteoarthritic symptoms, but only I knew the underlying cause. I had been forcing my legs to carry my body in a direction it didn't want to go, and now, no longer able to bear the awesome burden, my right hip joint had rebelled.

I awoke from the anesthesia in a plaster body cast that extended from my chest to my toes. I was fortunate in one respect: I had a sprightly Swiss nurse who would pop her head into my hospital room each morning and say, "Well there you are, safe and sound inside your cocoon. Who do you think you'll be when you emerge?"

I spent six months inside that cocoon, shedding my skin, waiting for my bones to mend. For the first few weeks I wanted nothing so much as to stand upright, to feel moving air against my body, but I was trapped in a place where the sun never shone, where the wind never blew. The physicians paraded in and out of my room, thumping my cast, as if they could tell by their hollow knock what was happening to the immobile man inside.

Nights were the worst, and it was during one of my sleepless spells—I didn't even have the luxury of tossing and turning—that the night heron returned. I would like to suggest something mystical—that he appeared in full plumage at the foot of my bed and spoke to me. But that wouldn't be true; in fact, it would detract from the truth, for I believe the graven images that etch themselves in our memory are more genuine than the ones we see, or think we see, in the murky woods or misty sky.

No, the bird wasn't sitting on my bed; he was perched exactly as I first saw him atop my mast, motionless, watching the still waters, waiting in the dead calm for the rise of a new wind. I remembered how I waited with him and how I was rewarded for my patience with a gentle, nudging breeze that filled my sails and carried me home.

Day after day, as I lay in my enforced idleness, I thought deeply about who I was, where I came from, and what I wanted to be. What I had lost in physical motion I had gained in insight, which is movement of another kind. I learned the interior life was as rewarding as the exterior life and that my richest moments occurred when I was absolutely still.

My bones knit; my body healed. As the day neared to cut me out of my cast, I knew I was well, because I was filled with a firm resolve. I had been chasing a material goal for its own sake, or perhaps because it was what I mistakenly thought my family, my friends, my colleagues—as well as a whole judgmental universe of faceless people—expected of me. As a result, I had lost the sense of myself, of what I had been put on earth to do.

From the time I was old enough to read, and possibly before, I had heard the music of language

79
·
first
you
have
to
row
a
little
boat

singing in my head. I was intrigued by the sound of words, by their cadence and by the images they formed in the books I read, and so it was inevitable that, as soon as I learned how, I started to string sentences together so I could let others know what I thought and felt. That was my talent; it was no better or worse than the talent possessed by others, but it was distinctly my own.

It is a strange and sad commentary that a man enters adult life wanting to be a poet and ends up in public relations. But I have to be careful where I place the blame for veering so far off course. It wasn't what others had done to me; it was what I had done to myself. Instead of pursuing my dream, I was ghostwriting articles and speeches for businessmen who had neither time nor inclination to speak for themselves. I lived close to the sources of corporate power, a seductive and flattering place to be, and I was highly compensated for what I did.

But it was vanity of vanities—and I paid a terrible price. I woke up each morning exhausted, dreading the thought of going to work, pushing myself against my will, dressing in a pinstripe suit I despised, boarding a commuter train to a city I hated, where I performed a function that aggrandized others and demeaned me. I was caught in a punishing wind and scared to death it might stop.

I pressed on until one day my hip caved in, my body collapsed, and I wound up immobilized, sunk in despair, not yet knowing I had brought this immobility upon myself because what I craved, more than security, more than success, was a dread calm that brings a new wind from a different shore. As I lay perfectly still, grappling with the nightmare death-in-life, which is a death worse than death itself, which was the death I had been living, I found the desire, the will that goes beyond mere acts of courage, to do what I had to do so that I might become the man I was meant to be.

It was midsummer when the doctors lifted me out of my cast; by fall, my strength and mobility had returned. I lived inland at that time, too far from the sea to celebrate my recovery with a sail, but I did the next best thing. I dug a hole in the backyard and planted a sapling, a sturdy red oak, and when spring came it blossomed nicely and the wind blew through its leaves.

81
·
first
you
have
to
row
a
little
boat

TEN

·

UNFOUNDED FEARS

·

I remember the first time I encountered the *Miss Ocean Beach* plowing through the bay, raising a wake higher than the highest waves on a stormy day. I was sitting under the boom, tiller over my shoulder, lost in thought, when suddenly there she was dead ahead on collision course, blaring her fearsome horn at me to get out of her way. The blast alone nearly pitched me overboard.

I scrambled to my feet as the speedy, low-slung ferry swept past to starboard with barely a hundred feet to spare. She was riding with her bow high and her stern low, cutting a broad swath in her passage down the channel that ran between Fire Island and Bay Shore. She had been a rumrunner during Prohibition days, and she still raced through the dredged waterways as if she was laden with contraband and a Coast Guard cutter in pursuit. Only now, instead of bootlegging liquor, she was carrying passengers who were milling about, gaping over the rails, amused (I imagined) by the near miss and waiting to see if I would survive the huge wake that was bearing down on me.

Had I done nothing, the mountainous swells would have struck me in the worst possible way: broadside. Fortunately I had sufficient presence of mind to turn my bow and hit them head on. The sails shook and the rigging rattled as my sloop rode the roller coaster, diving down the first wave, plunging through the second, and climbing the third. The boat emerged unscathed, but I was shaken to the core of my being, and for days afterward I heard the ferry's monster horn reverberating in my ears.

I made a solemn vow: Never again would I let another boat get that close to my hull. I kept a sharp eye out, and as soon as I spotted a vessel I would tack, jibe, do whatever I had to do to make sure we didn't collide. The other boat might be no more than a pinpoint on the horizon; it didn't matter. I would start to maneuver, certain that if I didn't take preventive measures at once we would both arrive at the same place at the same time.

85
·
first
you
have
to
row
a
little
boat

And then one day the inevitable occurred, something I should have foreseen but didn't because my judgment was skewered by my fright. While sailing upwind, I glanced under the boom and saw a fishing trawler with a flying bridge going full throttle, apparently aiming straight for me. Even though she was still a half mile away, I veered off to make sure I would safely cross her stern, but at the same moment she also turned, and we were once more on what seemed like a collision course. I tacked, keeping her in view, and in that instant struck a huge floating log directly under my bow.

The blue sloop shuddered on impact and I knew from the hard crunch that I had staved in the hull. I knelt on the floorboards and peered under the deck. Although it was too dark to see clearly, I could plainly hear the water sloshing through the gaping hole into the bilge. My boat came up into the wind, foundering. I quickly lowered the jib and, standing on the forward deck, waved my arms frantically. The trawler, the very one I had been trying to avoid, was now within a few hundred yards, and the owner, seeing my distress, cut his engine and called, "Are you all right?"

"I'm taking water!"

He brought his trawler as close to my boat as he could and threw me a line, which I secured around the base of the mast. A moment later I was standing on the stern of the fishing boat, heading for shore with my sloop in tow. She was listing dangerously but somehow managing to stay afloat. When we arrived at the shipyard, the workers promptly hauled her out, knocked the wooden plug out of her bottom, and drained her dry.

The captain, seeing the blue sloop up on the ways, rowed across the narrow creek between his home and the yard. He ran his hand over the splintered hull, rubbed his chin, and then looked at me.

"What happened?"

I told him the truth—that I was so busy watching the fishing boat way off in the distance that I didn't see the floating log right under my bow.

I thought he might lecture me then and there about flotsam and jetsam, shoals and flats, cans and nuns—all the dangers lurking in the water that can loom suddenly and wreck a ship. But instead, he said, "Well, don't you worry none. Archie here— he's the best mechanic you ever saw, and he'll fix up a plank and fit it in so it won't ever seem like anything happened at all."

Archie was the ship's carpenter at the yard, but the captain always referred to him as "the best mechanic you ever saw"—and his faith in the man's skill wasn't misplaced. A week later my boat was back in the water with a new plank in her bow and

a fresh coat of blue paint (which I had applied myself) on her hull. But even though the sloop was
ready to go, the sailor was not.

I stood on the shore, looking at my sloop, thinking
about all the terrible things that might happen to
me, and for a while I wasn't sure if I wanted to leave
the harbor. For the truth is that to sail, to even
contemplate sailing, calls for a fundamental faith in
one's self, and at that moment I was aware only of
the barriers between myself and my destination, a
patch of sandy beach on the other side of the bay.
First, I would have to tack out of the shipyard's basin
without crashing into the bulkhead, and then I would
have to negotiate eight miles of open water against
buffeting winds and battering waves.

Finally, I summoned up enough courage to board
my boat. I raised my sails, caught a puff, and began
my zigzag course up the saltwater creek, making the
best use of the fluky breeze that warped around
the houses and sheds that lined the shore. When I
reached the mouth of the creek, I trimmed my
sheets; the boat heeled, and all at once I was free of
land, pointing into the wind, aiming straight for the
water tower glistening in the sun above the beach
community of Saltaire.

Two-thirds of the way across I saw a massive
tanker barreling through the channel, heading for
the oil terminal in Patchogue, twenty miles away.
She was riding low in the water, moving inexorably
toward her destination, making it plain by her reso-

87
•
first
you
have
to
row
a
little
boat

lute passage that she wasn't about to be deterred by any craft, small or large, that got in her way. Afraid I might run into her, I decided to head up into the wind, to come to a complete halt and wait for her to pass. But just as I was about to dump the wind out of my sails, I caught myself.

Why do that? I thought. She's still a long way off.

I continued to sail, and as I approached the tanker it became obvious we wouldn't collide. She was going to cross my bow, leaving plenty of sea between us. I would still have to contend with her wake, but if I held to my present course with the wind full in my sails, the thrust of my sloop would carry me safely by.

It happened exactly that way; the tanker and I missed each other by a wide margin, and as we went our separate ways I realized I had been squandering a tremendous amount of energy fretting about a future that wasn't there. I had to be vigilant, to make mental note of the vessel, to recognize she was out there somewhere, a potential hazard. But I also had to guard against reacting too soon, because the vision of disaster that rose so vividly in my mind might turn out to be nothing more than an unfounded fear.

As I crossed the tanker's wake, my apprehensions began to fade. Although I didn't know it at the time, I was taking my first tentative steps toward becoming a master not so much of my boat or of myself but of reality. I was learning that before giving way to a seemingly threatening object I would have to sail close enough to it to find out what it was, where it was going, and if it would do me harm. Then, and only then, could I decide whether to veer off, head up, or sail on.

I was also acquiring a personal perspective about the world in which I dwelt. My guardian aunt liked to preach that "everything happens for the best"— a dictum in which she firmly believed, as if there were a hidden hand guiding human destiny. But I was discovering as I sailed that the universe was indifferent to my plight and I couldn't predict before I left the safety of the harbor what obstacles I might encounter on the bay. I couldn't foresee when a ferry would come out of nowhere and blare its horn at me or when my boat would ram a log floating randomly in the sea. Even those purportedly consistent elements of nature—wind, waves, and tides— seemed to defy the desperate forecasts of man and take on a turbulence of their own.

The distant shoreline with its coves and points appeared as irregular, as richly varied, as the lobes of a maple leaf. The herring gulls drifting haphazardly across the summer sky settled like snowflakes on the beach. The grebes swimming off my bow arched their backs and dove without warning, popping up at random places on the surface and suddenly diving again. If there was a pattern to all these indiscriminate movements, I couldn't detect it, and I had to admit to myself I had no idea what would happen next.

89

•

first
you
have
to
row
a
little
boat

It was an unholy view, one that contradicted what I had been taught in Sunday school, and at first I was troubled by it. My religion teacher, a kindly woman who took a special interest in me, claimed that there was a grand design to the universe, that an all-knowing deity ruled heaven and earth with a purpose in mind. I wanted to believe her; it was a comfort to think that what she said was true. But the more I sailed, the more convinced I became that she deluded herself, that life was a lot more confused and chaotic than she dared to admit.

In science class I was told that the physical world was governed by immutable laws. My chemistry teacher described how electrons orbited the nucleus of an atom in the same predictable way the planets circled the sun. A stern disciplinarian who taught by rote, he believed that science could answer all the nagging questions of existence raised by man. But with the passage of time I discovered science had its shortcomings, too. It could tell me how fluids behaved under pressure or how air moved across the surface of a sail or wing. But it couldn't tell me where to go or what to do or how to get from where I was to where I wanted to be.

And yet if the universe was an uncertain place, I wasn't unduly perturbed. I didn't demand a mechanistic view of the solar system to feel at home in my small corner of the globe. I sailed the Great South Bay, watching for a changing wind or a flattening sea. I exercised my skills, taking pleasure in the unpredictable, erratic aspect of nature, feeling comfortable with myself because I had learned how to cope with surprise. Gradually, I came to understand that if there was an order to my life it was one I imposed through what I practiced and what I perceived.

As I grew older and more experienced, I realized that the ability to distinguish between real and apparent dangers is fundamental to good judgment, and people who don't possess it are seriously handicapped. They dwell in a state of incipient catastrophe, thinking only of what can go wrong and trying to ward it off before it occurs. They aren't masters of reality, although they like to think they are; they're masters of unreality because they let their fears, which are figments of an untrustworthy imagination, govern their lives. It's as if they never break through a secret barrier that separates the timorous from the self-assured.

I know a brilliant attorney who plans family outings with the same diligence he tries cases in a court of law. To the consternation of his wife and children, he insists on preparing for every possible contingency, every imaginable disaster, before they leave. Life for him is a trial, a real trial, and he is in a constant adversarial relationship with it, trying to beat it at its own game. In so doing he misses out on the simple, unexpected pleasures of the moment at hand.

I know a housewife who betrays her fright by

91
•
first
you
have
to
row
a
little
boat

trying to plan every activity in advance. Her husband says he can set his watch by what she is doing at any given moment of the day. Is she throwing laundry into the washing machine? Then it must be Tuesday morning at ten. Is she heading for the supermarket? Then it must be Thursday afternoon at two. She serves dinner every evening promptly at six (not at one minute past) so she can be cleaned up in time for television at seven. Every night she rises from her living room chair promptly at ten and goes to bed.

People like that are more common than we suppose, and it's unfortunate, because the spirit of adventure lies dormant in their veins, and those who know them live with the futile hope that they will somehow get it stirring again. But they rarely do, for the simple reason that they can't afford to let the world get out of their control. But the world can't be controlled; it's patently not controllable—that's the only physical principle I know for sure. Rather than face up to that reality, they withdraw, and the sadness is that with each passing day they retreat a little further into their circumscribed world.

Years ago, when I commuted to a nine-to-five job, I often lunched with a colleague who saw a conspiracy behind every event—from the assassination of President Kennedy to the mysterious disappearance of his car keys. He was sure the Central Intelligence Agency was behind one and burglars behind the other. He couldn't accept the idea that

93
·
first
you
have
to
row
a
little
boat

sometimes history happens—that a random killer can lock himself in a book depository with a rifle or a distracted executive can drop his keys in the snow. He needed an explanation for the unexplainable, an assurance that there was an intelligent mind behind every occurrence, no matter how ominous it might be—and so he preferred the illusion of conspiracy to the reality of happenstance. In due course his paranoia took over his life. First, he lost his job, then his wife; but, of course, he viewed those events as part of a grand conspiracy, too.

We live in a world that is so chaotic that we have come to believe only a machine with electronic circuits can cope with the variables. We build mathematical models and we stuff them into those machines so they can tell us what we think we want to know. We ask the machines to answer ultimate "what if" questions: What if interest rates climb through the roof? What if the sun falls out of the sky? And the machines tell us and we use the answers to turn a knob here or throw a switch there. But there's a major flaw in this approach, apart from the fact that it works only some of the time, and it's that we have become so busy preventing the future that there's never a now.

It may well be, as I think about it, that the prime virtue of my blue sloop was that it compelled me to live in the present and to avoid too much unhealthy speculation about what might happen at some indefinite point ahead which I couldn't plainly see. For the truth is that I already know as much about my fate as I need to know. The day will come when I will die. So the only matter of consequence before me is what I will do with my allotted time. I can remain on shore, paralyzed with fear, or I can raise my sails and dip and soar in the breeze.

E L E V E N

.

F O G B O U N D

.

One morning I tacked out of the harbor under a sky so clear I thought I could reach out and touch each separate leaf along the shore. It was one of those deceptive summer days that conveys no hint of the storm to come. I scooped up a bucket of water and doused my head—to feel the salt on my face, its taste on my tongue.

It wasn't until late in the day while I was skimming the barrier beach that I saw the thunderheads far out to sea. The black sky curled back on itself, like a tidal wave rolling inexorably toward shore. I aimed for the boat basin at Ocean Beach, shot through the narrow opening, and came up to a mooring post on the lee side of the wharf. My sails were luffing so fiercely I thought they might shred. I lowered them quickly and stuffed them under the deck just ahead of the driving rain.

I spent that night wrapped in damp sails under the sloop's protective cuddy, occasionally dozing but mostly listening to the wind in the rigging, the sound of the halyards slapping the mast. In that fitful half-world between wakefulness and sleep, the past rose up and overwhelmed me, and I remembered the life I had, the life I lost, the life that was no more. I saw my father sitting at his easel beside floor-to-ceiling windows in our Manhattan apartment overlooking the Hudson River and he was painting—painting vivid scenes of Moorish harbors and Arabian marts, painting white birches and the rocky ledges of the Maine coast, painting an Indian squaw holding her papoose, both wrapped in a long red shawl, painting a lateen-rigged dhow floating off the white coast of Africa—and I was across the studio from him, sprawled on a chaise, gazing at images rising like ghosts from his drawing board.

I have no idea if such inclinations are inherited,

97

•

first
you
have
to
row
a
little
boat

but I like to believe my father passed his romantic leanings on to me, and I delved deeply into myself in a desperate attempt to restore those tenuous threads that bind a father to his son. My uncle was good to me; he provided me with food, with shelter, with a beautiful blue sloop, and he granted me the freedom to sail, but he lacked my father's artistic passion and intensity, and those were precisely the qualities that haunted me at that indecisive moment of my life.

I awoke at dawn. The wind had let up and the rain stopped, but a dense fog shrouded the bay—a fog so thick it had crept into every cranny, every crevice along the quay. I was hungry and cold and feeling desperately alone, and so I decided to chance it, to run the twelve miles home by dead reckoning, feeling my way as best I could across the bay.

I swept past black cans and red nuns, but halfway between the barrier beach and the mainland I came to know the penetrating fear of fog. The mist was so heavy I could barely make out the mast in front of me. I might be sailing in circles; I might be heading away from Bay Shore back toward Fire Island. I might be slipping past the lighthouse, out the treacherous inlet into the Atlantic. I might be heading for Sayville, a mainland hamlet as good as a million miles from my desired landfall.

I continued to sail, not knowing if I was about to run aground or ram a channel marker or another boat anchored off my bow. I had no idea where I was heading, but in that dim, bewildering world I believed my only salvation was to keep moving, moving somewhere, moving anywhere, even though my sense of direction had deserted me. And then from the impenetrable core of the mist I heard the captain's voice coming at me clear as a warning horn, repeating something he had told me during one of my early sailing lessons when I pushed the tiller the wrong way and almost threw the boat into a dangerous jibe.

"Let go of the tiller!" he was saying. "Just let go of the tiller! Don't try to steer when you're confused!"

I followed his advice and the blue sloop did exactly what she was supposed to do. She nudged up gently into the breeze and came to a standstill. I went up on the bow and tossed the anchor overboard and sat on the foredeck, waiting for a revelation, a glimmer of light, to tell me where I was and which way I had to go.

Deep in the center of that fog there was no shoreline, no guiding star, no rising sun, no setting moon. But I had enough sailing experience by then to know that if I studied the elements carefully I would discover a clue that would put the muddled compass of my mind back in working order. What I had to do was sit calmly on the deck and empty my mind of all its preconceived notions and prejudices about the nature of fog, and then I would be able to detect the one constant in the swirling mist that would set me on my rightful course.

It was out there, I was sure it was, but for all my concentration it refused to appear. And then all at once I remembered that a boat at anchor, like a gull on a post, is a weather vane; it points into the wind, and when I knew that I also knew what I was looking for and why it had eluded me. I had been peering into the fog, searching the most obscure place, as if the solution was hidden from view, when in fact it was self-evident, and that was exactly the attribute that made it so hard to find.

It was the wind, and I knew by its moist touch, by its scent, by its speed that it was still blowing as it had been blowing all morning—from the east. I hauled anchor and caught a puff in my jib; I steered sideways to the breeze and, sailing a broad reach, headed north toward home.

An hour later I saw the white rim of the sun burning through the fog. A gull passed overhead, and under its wing I saw the faint trace of shore; then the whitewashed walls of a beach and cabana club loomed beside the head of the harbor, barely a hundred yards away. I had done a foolish thing; I should have waited at the barrier beach for the fog to lift, but I had made my way across the shallows and flats, guided only by my sense of direction, which came from the wind.

I know now, in the reflection of years, that I was

99

•

first
you
have
to
row
a
little
boat

bound by fog long before I learned to sail. In the aftermath of my parents' death I had vowed never to love again, for to love was to risk more than I could bear to lose. I had pushed my sadness so far down into the base of my being that I didn't even know it was there. Death does that to us; it's so irrevocable, so absolute, we would rather deny its existence than face up to our sorrow and pass through our pain.

But I believe we are born with a power to heal our wounds, not through miracles but through a silent voice that speaks to us from within ourselves and won't be stilled, a voice that tells us where to go and what to do, which is a miracle of another kind. It is the refusal to heed that inner voice that causes the incurable sickness of the soul which makes us wither before our time.

In my loneliness I turned intuitively toward my sloop, which was the gift of life that saved me from myself. Through sailing I discovered the generous nature of my surrogate parents, found gainful employment with Ed Doubrava, gathered in the seafaring wisdom of the captain, befriended shipyard workers and clam diggers and ferryboat skippers, met the boys who became my friends and the woman who would become my wife and the mother of my children.

And yet there were moments in those castaway days of my youth when I secretly envied the seeming certainty of the boys and girls I knew. They dwelt

101

•

first
you
have
to
row
a
little
boat

with their own parents in their own homes and they never questioned their origins or where they belonged. They traveled in cliques—went to parties and dances in cliques and congregated in cliques in the school corridors and cafeteria. They knew nothing of the well of alienation that can rise and overwhelm a life.

I distinctly remember the leader of one of the cliques, the supremely confident captain of the football team, a hard-bitten runner who put his helmeted head down and bowled over any would-be tackler in his path. He owned a jalopy and sometimes after practice he deigned to drive me home. Each time he inevitably asked me the same question—whether my mother and father ever attended the Saturday games to watch me play.

It was a painful question, and I could have taken the easy way out, answering no and letting it go at that. But I felt compelled to say what I had to say because my identity was at stake, and so each time he raised the subject I told him I lived with my aunt and uncle because my parents were dead. He never commented; it was as if he hadn't heard. At first I thought the facts embarrassed him, but after a while I realized they simply hadn't registered; he couldn't grasp that the circumstances of my family life differed from his.

With the passage of time I came to see that this penchant for running roughshod over others is often mistaken for leadership and that individuals adept at it tend to rise to positions of power. But the truth is that they're usually more fogbound than those beset by self-doubt. When faced with a crisis—a Watergate break-in or an Alaskan oil spill or a Bhopal gas leak—they call in their consultants, who tell them what to think, and their speechwriters, who tell them what to say, because they're totally incapable of identifying with the plight of others or comprehending how they feel.

I've grown distrustful of people who are dead certain; they're inept at best and dangerous at worst because their vision is circumscribed by what they think they know. They are like the befogged Monsieur G——, the Prefect of the Parisian police in "The Purloined Letter" by Edgar Allan Poe, who can't see the stolen document he's searching for even though it's staring him in the face. And why can't he see it? Because he assumes the thief did exactly what he would do with a pilfered letter: hide it in some obscure place. And so the Prefect wastes weeks probing cushions, mattresses, carpets—he even inspects table and floor joints with a microscope—all in a futile attempt to find an envelope that the culprit has artfully concealed on his mantelpiece.

At length, Monsieur G——takes his problem to the astute C. Auguste Dupin (the first in a long line of mythic sleuths who inhabit our literature), interrupting a session of "meditation and a meerschaum," a mixture which hasn't impaired the detective's mental acuity. Dupin concludes correctly, even before he visits the culprit's premises, that the letter isn't hidden, at least not in the conventional sense, and he twits the Prefect for his myopia:

> "Perhaps the mystery is a little *too* plain," said Dupin.
> "Oh, good heavens! who ever heard of such an idea?"
> "A little *too* self-evident."
> "Ha! ha! ha!—ha! ha! ha!—ho! ho! ho! . . . oh, Dupin, you will be the death of me yet!"

Dupin finds the letter at once, not because he's observant but because he's perceptive; he looks through the letter, beyond the letter into the devious heart of the thief himself, and there he sees what the Prefect can't see and will never see no matter how long and hard he looks. It's not surprising that the detectives we hold in high esteem—Sherlock Holmes, Hercule Poirot, Miss Marple, Nero Wolfe, Charlie Chan, Lieutenant Columbo—all possess this uncanny ability to see the obvious. We admire them, we say, for their powers of deduction—but detection isn't deduction; it's something else: the ability to examine the evidence the world presents with an unfettered mind.

I search for the source of fog and I find it everywhere. It rises at dew point in the valley, settles on the hilltop, and blows in from the sea like a huge

103
•
first
you
have
to
row
a
little
boat

cloud that hugs the land. Unlike the tide, it abides by no timetable but ebbs and flows in compliance with its own mysterious clockwork, casting its primal spell over all it touches, transfiguring the landscape we thought we knew.

I was a young man when I married, and with the fervor of youth I told myself, This bond will last forever, but I was wrong. Three decades after my marriage began, it ended, and even though that ending was what I sought, what I wanted, I once again found myself bound by fog, this time through divorce, which is death of another kind. In some ways it's even worse, for in death we know the ones we love are physically gone, but in divorce they're still with us, reminding us of the shared life that went awry. And yet the separation is just as shattering, and it's the acute pain of separation that casts us into that lost world.

In the dim days after my wife and I parted, I found myself caught in fog so permanent, so pervasive that I thought it would never lift. I thrashed about, moving from one liaison to another, unable to forge a genuine attachment, unable to make even the most basic decisions about where to eat or what to wear without continually changing my mind. Trapped in my own private miasma, I spent one entire day driving back and forth between two car dealers ten miles apart, trying to figure out if I wanted the station wagon at one or the hatchback at the other—until at last I pulled over to the side of the road and slumped down in the seat, exhausted by the ordeal.

And then I remembered that harrowing morning halfway between the mainland and the barrier beach when I sat on the deck of my blue sloop, staring into the mist—and I knew what I had to do. I found myself a cottage beside the sea, where I lived alone for three years, watching for that breath of air that would tell me what I wanted and where I was supposed to go. In due course it came, and when it did I recognized it at once as the favorable breeze I was waiting for, and I let it carry me toward companionship, toward love, toward a new coast and the work I wanted to do.

I am sorry for those individuals who are unsighted, but I am sorrier still for those sighted people who have lost their bearings, for they are truly blind. Unable to see, they steer without purpose, without direction until they founder and disappear. Whenever I feel myself slipping into that hopeless state, as I sometimes do, I remember the words of the captain, uttered so long ago, and I let go of the tiller and head up into the wind.

105

•

first
you
have
to
row
a
little
boat

TWELVE

·

OF KNOTS, LOOPS,

BENDS, AND HITCHES

·

*B*efore I learned to sail I thought a knot was any old lump in a rope, but Ed Doubrava taught me otherwise on the very first day I journeyed with him across the bay. He had maneuvered his powerboat, *Jove,* up to a rickety dock at Oak Island and ordered me to jump ashore with the bow line in my hand. I landed safely and promptly began to wrap the hawser around a mooring post, winding it and winding it and finally tying the standing parts into the worst tangle imaginable.

When Ed saw the mess I had made, he undid it and deftly dropped two symmetrical loops—one on top of the other—over the post and pulled them taut.

"That's the best way to secure a line to a post," he said. "It only takes a second and it won't jam— no matter how hard the boat pulls against it."

To prove his point, he undid the knot easily, even though it was under considerable stress, and handed the line to me. The first time I tried to tie the same knot I turned the top loop the wrong way, and the line slipped off the post when I gave it a tug. I tried again, this time making sure the loops were identical, and dropped them over the post, first one and then the other. When I finished the wind caught *Jove* broadside and blew it away from the dock; for an instant I thought the boat might carry across the creek, but the bow line pulled taut and the knot held.

I stood on the pier looking at the folded strands, at the impeccable way they lapped the post. The knot was so simple, yet so elegant for its simplicity. Two loops, that's all it was—two loops surrounding a post with the standing parts tucked between them, emerging in opposite directions, an arrangement of forces so well conceived and so artistically pleasing that it was hard to believe it was also practical.

Ed hadn't said to me, "Now I'm going to teach you the clove hitch"—and it wasn't until I came across a picture of it in an encyclopedia of knots that I learned its name. The manual had a convoluted description that said nothing about dropping two loops over a post. I tried to decipher the drawing, but the longer I studied it the more confused I became, and a cynical notion entered my head. It struck me that every clam digger and party-boat captain on the Great South Bay knew a better way to tie the clove hitch than the authority who prepared the text.

I had found the encyclopedia at a book sale; since it was cheap, I bought it. But I used it only as a secondary source to verify the names of the loops, bends, and hitches I learned from baymen who knew exactly how to tie the knots—even if they didn't always know what they were called. Ed added two half hitches to my repertoire, a handy alternate to the clove hitch. The captain contributed the figure eight, which I tied at the ends of my sheets to prevent them from slipping through their sheaves; the bowline, a stable loop which I kept around my mooring post in the harbor; and the sheet bend, a reliable way to join two ropes of different thickness.

One day, a weather-beaten, squinty-eyed shipyard worker named Simmy Baker saw me whipping halyard ends so they wouldn't unravel and he showed me how to interweave the strands instead. A homespun man with homespun solutions, he put the com-

109

•

first
you
have
to
row
a
little
boat

pleted splice under the thick sole of his shoe and performed a fancy step he called the "stomp and roll" to press the loose ends snugly together. I searched but found no mention of Simmy's dance in my encyclopedia.

I worked at these knots until I had them fixed in my brain and could tie them with my eyes closed. They were so ingenious that I couldn't help but wonder where they came from. A good knot, it seemed to me, was like a cherished folk song; it was passed down from parent to child to grandchild until it became part of the lore of the race and its author was lost to history.

I try to remember who taught me the square knot, the grandfather of all knots, and I suddenly realize it was my mother when she showed me how to tie the laces on my shoes. A variant of that familiar bow, it originated with sailors of yore who used it to secure a reefed, or shortened, sail so they could weather a storm. Its utility proved so great that it gradually made its way into the public domain where it exists today as ambient knowledge, free to anyone who wants to find out how it works.

The square knot consists of two overhand knots pulled firmly together—and yet it's remarkable how easy it is to go astray. Cross the ends of the second knot the wrong way and we get a "granny," an ugly affair that jams, especially when wet; in a crisis, it must be cut with a knife, a stiff penalty for such a small mistake. Cross the ends the right way and we get the knot we want, a knot of character that bears no resemblance to the "granny" in the way it looks or behaves.

My encyclopedia warns me against the square knot, saying it isn't as trustworthy as it seems—an inadvertent bump or a wrong twist and it's likely to jiggle loose. Nevertheless, I've relied on it countless times throughout my life and it has never let me down. When I was a boy I thought of it as just another handy knot, but as I grew older I found myself tying it for the pleasure of looking at it, the way one might look into the churning wake behind a boat, with hypnotic wonder, for the subtle meanings hidden there.

I reach out and grab the draw cord that dangles from the window shade above my desk. Whenever I want to amuse myself, divert myself from the tedium of words, I tie a knot in the draw cord just for the sake of seeing how it goes together and comes undone. I tie a square knot, making sure the end that crosses on top of the first overhand knot also crosses on top of the second. I pull it closed, slide it open, pull it closed. It never slips, never jams, and as I work the knot back and forth, open and closed, I see an image, a sensual image I never saw before.

I see a perfect symbol for the union of male and female, man and woman, husband and wife—for their lovemaking and leave-taking, their urge to be joined and their need to be apart. When I tighten the knot, I see entangled lovers, their limbs wrapped

111
•
first
you
have
to
row
a
little
boat

around each other, their legs outstretched. When I loosen the knot, I see the lovers letting go, the way they must, for lovers—no matter how devoted—can't be bound by their love every moment of their lives.

Yet all too often when a man and a woman come together they don't tie a square knot; they tie a "granny," and so they're less like partners than prisoners of love. They scrape and chafe against each other, but no matter how they struggle they can't escape their bonds. "We're getting hitched," we hear them say as they head for the altar, and their words are more prophetic than they know. Once wed, they march in lockstep at the same pace, at the same gait, with the same hitch to their stride. It's a sorry state, but it can't be helped; since the knot they tied won't loosen, they wind up strangling themselves.

I think of the Gordian knot, a tangle so intricate that its solution defied the brightest minds of ancient Greece—until Alexander the Great rode out of Macedonia. Alexander didn't untie the knot; he sliced it with his sword—and with that bold stroke, according to legend, earned the right to conquer Asia, which he did, slaughtering and enslaving as he went. Ever since, this clever king—part man, part god—has been acclaimed for his audacity, but to my mind the meaning of the myth lies elsewhere. It says that a knot which can't be undone ultimately leads to human misery.

I reach again for the draw cord and tie a bowline,

a small loop in part of the rope, and then I pass the end through it: under, over, around and back through. I tie the sheet bend, and I'm surprised at how similar the motions are to the bowline: under, over, around and back again. I turn the high stool on which I sit upside down and tie a clove hitch and then two half hitches around an upright leg. I tie a figure eight and then a square knot, and I am filled with a sense of completeness that comes from knowing the skills I acquired when I was a youth are with me still.

Six knots, that's all—six knots, each entrenched in my psyche, each with an unexplored myth of its own—and I know there are thousands of others, so many untold knots, like so many unread books, that in my lifetime I couldn't begin to know them all. And so I content myself with these six, for they are the ones I need the most when I go down to the sea and raise my sails.

113

·

first
you
have
to
row
a
little
boat

THIRTEEN

·

A FORGIVING BOAT

·

Tiny West Island rises like a jewel in the Great South Bay about a mile north of the barrier beach, and its most prominent feature when I was a boy was a battered house that had been bowled off its stilts by a hurricane. It perched precariously on the edge of the reedy shore, its front porch partially submerged and its shingles weathered and warped by wind and rain. I had seen it many times, always from a distance, always with curiosity, but one day I decided to sail as close to it as possible for a better look.

I skimmed the shoals, confident of my ability to "read" the water, but the tide was ebbing faster than I thought and I miscalculated. The keel struck a sandbar and the sloop came to an abrupt halt, listing to leeward; even though the wind filled the sails, she stuck fast. I jumped overboard (the water barely came to the bottom of my bathing suit), pressed my shoulder against the bow, and pushed it toward deeper water, and then—as the sloop gained speed—clambered aboard and sailed away.

There's no sound like water slurping under the hull of a boat which only moments before was hard aground. I considered myself fortunate; if I hadn't dislodged her, I might've spent the next six hours high and dry, waiting for the tide to turn and float me free. I told myself there had to be a better way, a handy warning system to prevent the same thing from happening again, but I didn't know what it was. I had heard of electronic depth-finders; I vaguely knew there were such gizmos, but it never occurred to me to equip my simple sloop with such an alien device.

Then one drizzly day while wandering about the shipyard, I bumped into Simmy Baker and told him how I had accidentally grounded my boat on a sand-

117

•

first
you
have
to
row
a
little
boat

bar off West Island. Simmy had been a rumrunner in Prohibition days (at least that was the scuttlebutt about old Bay Shore) and that made him a hero in my youthful eyes. A rumrunner, I figured, had to know more than anyone else about how to slip through shoals and flats, and I was hoping he would pass some of his smuggler's lore on to me. While I told him my tale, he scanned the sky as if he was searching for a sign of clearing, and when I finished he fixed his gaze on me.

"That boat of yours," he said, "she has a centerboard as well as a keel, doesn't she?"

"Yes, she does," I replied, not sure what he was driving at. My blue sloop was a hybrid creature, designed expressly for the shallow waters of the Great South Bay. Most sailing vessels have either an adjustable centerboard (literally, a vertical board in the center of the boat) that can be raised or lowered from the cockpit or a keel that is fixed in place under the hull. But my boat had a combination of both: a keel that drew two and a half feet of water, and a centerboard that dropped through a slot in the keel to provide another foot of stability when the water was deep enough—which it rarely was.

"But I'll bet you never use it," Simmy said.

He was absolutely right. "I don't need it," I said. "It's a nuisance."

"Maybe so," he said, "maybe so. But if she was my boat, I'd drop that centerboard as soon as I raised my sails."

The next time I tacked out of the long, narrow canal, I took his advice, and I noticed at once that my sloop was slipping sideways less than when the board was up, and so making better headway. In the past I needed at least ten tacks to clear the mouth of the canal; now I needed only eight. When I reached open water, the difference was even more dramatic. Usually when beating against the prevailing southwesterly, the best I could do was aim for the silvery water tower glistening above Saltaire; now I could head straight for the Fire Island Light, a compass point or two closer to the wind.

As I neared West Island, I saw the deserted beach house teetering on the marshy bank amid the cattails, and I was drawn toward the mysterious dwelling with its lopsided porch, half awash, by a power beyond myself, a power only a boy can know. I had no choice; I had to negotiate the shallows, test myself against the shoals and flats one more time. The tide was in, and that helped me sail within a few hundred feet of the shore, much closer than I had thought possible. Suddenly I heard a thump; for an instant I thought my boat had struck bottom. I was about to jump overboard to push her free when I realized that she wasn't docked in sand—that she was still nudging ahead even though her forward progress was seriously impeded.

I heard the thump again and then again, and all at once I knew exactly where the noise was coming from. It was the centerboard bouncing off the bay

119
•
first
you
have
to
row
a
little
boat

bottom, popping up through the cockpit trunk and bouncing off the bottom again. It was sending me a signal as undeniably certain as any high-tech sounding device; it was warning me that a mere foot of water separated the sandbar from my keel.

I veered away from the island toward the channel; within a few moments, the thumping had stopped and the sloop was scooting freely with ample water under her hull. I steered slowly, carefully back toward the shoals; as soon as the centerboard began to bounce off the bottom, I headed up into the wind, tossed my anchor over the bow, dropped my jib, and waded ashore.

The house was boarded up, with a NO TRES-PASSING—UNDER PENALTY OF LAW sign tacked on the front door, an unnecessary affront since there was virtually no stable flooring left to walk on. I stood on the porch, balancing myself on a rotted beam, and studied the tattered notice, reading its warning over and over again: NO TRESPASSING—UNDER PEN-ALTY OF LAW. The words sounded so prohibitive, so relentlessly unforgiving that I couldn't believe they were meant for me. I had taken a tremendous risk; I had chanced running aground and damaging my hull, and now I had reached my destination only to discover that the absent owners, whoever they were, distrusted my presence. In their abject fear, they were ordering me to "Keep Out!"—as if I was a vandal from the sea bent on sacking what was left of their house.

A phrase from the Lord's Prayer popped into my head: "Forgive us our trespasses as we forgive those who trespass against us." Although I had been sent to Sunday school and made to recite those words in unison with others, I now had to acknowledge that I didn't have the slightest idea what they meant. To trespass was to sin—but what was it to trespass against another, and how calamitous would it be if I defied the judicial injunction, if I forced open the warped door and stepped inside? I was alone on the island. There was no one to witness my transgression. Who would ever know!

I pushed against the door with all my might, but it wouldn't budge; either it was too heavy or I was too weak. I tried again and felt the awesome weight, not of the swollen timbers but of the covenants and restrictions that governed my life. My way was barred. I should've been angry, but instead of fury I felt relief. It's just as well, I told myself. Suppose I got in and broke a leg. They'd blame me because I'm a trespasser—and trespassing is against the law.

I can feel the impact of that NO TRESPASSING sign as keenly now as on that day so long ago when I was struggling with all the invisible barriers, all the arbitrary boundaries I dared not cross. It seemed to me at that desolate moment as if the world in which I dwelt was a maze of artificial lines drawn by others to keep me in my place. But I know now that what prevented me, what has always prevented me, from doing what I wanted to do wasn't lack of brainpower or brute strength; it was my tacit acceptance of laws laid down by someone else.

My guardian aunt was one of the more ardent rule makers in my life, and I could hear her complaining voice coming to me clear across the bay.

"You left the light burning in your bedroom. Go upstairs and turn it out!"

"You left the water dripping in the bathtub. Please close the faucet tight!"

One morning I found a note taped to the mirror of the medicine cabinet above the sink. "Squeeze the toothpaste from the bottom," it said, "not from the top!"

A joke, I thought, it's just a joke—but later I discovered she was morally offended by the way I brushed my teeth.

Were all these deeds of mine trespasses? Judging from her reaction to them, I felt as if they were, as if I had violated her sense of the way things ought to be. And yet I had to concede this was petty stuff—that some of her rules actually made sense. It was a necessary condition of daily life that lights not be left burning in the bedroom or water dripping in the tub. I was irked less by the substance of her commandments than by the manner in which she handed them down.

I could rebel; I knew that. I could refuse to comply and go on squeezing the toothpaste from the top. I could fashion a battering ram and smash my way into this abandoned house. But rebellion wasn't in

121

•

first
you
have
to
row
a
little
boat

my nature; as much as I wanted to assert my independence, I recognized the futility of confrontation for its own sake. I had to find a saner way to sail, a more favorable angle to the wind.

I glanced across the water at my sloop, swaying at her anchor line, her mainsail luffing lightly in the breeze. She was like a faithful horse at a hitching post or a friend on a street corner, waiting patiently—without judgment, without reproach—for my return. I waded out, raised the foresail, hauled anchor, and steered a broad reach through the channel halfway between West Island and the barrier beach. I had been sailing for only a few minutes when I sensed there was something wrong and realized what it was. I had neglected Simmy's dictum; I hadn't lowered the centerboard.

I pulled out the pivot pin and the board slid down the trunk, through the keel and into the water, giving me an extra foot of draft. The sloop responded at once; she heeled over on her lines and revealed an aspect of her character I didn't know was there. If I trimmed my sail too tightly or let it out too far, she didn't threaten to capsize or come to a sudden stop; instead, she adjusted her course without making a fuss and continued to surge ahead, slicing through the sea. It was as if the sloop had a mind of her own, as if she were compensating for my mistakes, and doing it in a way that was so gentle, so considerate that I really didn't take umbrage at all.

123

•

first
you
have
to
row
a
little
boat

As I continued to sail, I saw many different kinds of boats and I studied them all to see how they compared with mine. There were beamy, lumbering, gaff-rigged catboats, as stable as any boat could be, yet seemingly immune to a shift of wind or change of tide. And there were small, sensitive racing Snipes, Comets, and Frostbite dinghies, which reacted to the slightest touch of the tiller or trim of sail. My blue sloop fell somewhere between those two extremes; she responded to the elements slowly, perceptibly in a way that gave me time to grasp what was going on.

The lessons of youth lie latent within us and inform our later years, and I feel safe in saying that the kind of boat I sailed as a boy influenced the sort of man I became. I know what I like and don't like in my dealings with others, and I believe I can trace my attitudes back to that crucial day when I first lowered my centerboard. I seek in friends, partners, and mates what I seek in a sloop: a forgiving relationship in which I automatically compensate for their shortcomings and they for mine.

Yet I know the subtle give and take I prefer is also the most difficult to find for the simple reason that so many people view forgiveness in an entirely unforgivable way. They see it as a struggle in which one party admits to wrongdoing and apologizes while the other party self-righteously accepts the admission and forgives. In such a relationship, the air is filled with endless recriminations and every act becomes a test of will, a tug-of-war.

Through my sailing years I never once apologized to my sloop and she never apologized to me, and I suspect that if I could have incarnated her as a human we would have adjusted to each other's foibles in the same respectful way. If I had left the light burning in the bedroom or the water dripping in the tub, she would have taken the appropriate corrective action without making any claim on me. As for the toothpaste tube, I think she would have let me squeeze it any way I chose.

Years later, long after I had left the Great South Bay, I found myself wandering through a harbor north of Seattle on Puget Sound, studying the boats docked along the shore. I came upon one, a seaworthy ketch, which appealed to me the moment I laid eyes on her. As I stood admiring her sheer, graceful lines, her owner emerged from the cabin and we struck up a conversation. He told me he lived aboard with his wife and ten-year-old daughter and the three of them had sailed the boat clear across the Pacific from her home port of Singapore.

He invited me down into her cabin and proceeded to show me every feature: her sturdy bunks, her tidy head, her compact galley, and her ample stowage space. I was duly impressed, especially with her mahogany joinery, but when we returned to the deck I didn't mention any of those things. Instead, I said, "She strikes me as a forgiving boat."

As soon as I uttered those words, he broke into a broad smile, as if I had paid him the highest compliment possible. I had no doubt he understood exactly what I meant.

"Yes, she is," he replied as we shook hands. "I wouldn't sail any other kind."

125

•

first
you
have
to
row
a
little
boat

FOURTEEN

·

A LAZY SAILOR AT HEART

·

One day, to my surprise, my aunt asked if I would take her for a sail. Up to then her interest in my sloop was marginal at best. She didn't interfere with my sailing; in fact, she encouraged it, but she never expressed a desire to board the boat herself.

I didn't want to take her. She was a

small, anxious woman given to making impromptu sermons, and I dreaded the thought of being trapped alone with her. I gave an evasive reply, hoping she would let the matter drop, but one morning she repeated her request with such insistence that I had no tactful way to refuse.

We sailed out of the harbor under a light breeze from the land; when we reached open water I didn't head across the bay, as was my custom, but deliberately hugged the mainland shore.

"It's quite safe along here," I said. "We won't capsize—but if we do you'll be able to stand on the bottom with no trouble at all."

"Oh, I'm not worried about tipping over," she said, and her voice sounded so calm that for an instant I wasn't sure it was hers. "You may not believe this," she went on, "but I was a strong swimmer when I was a girl."

"Were you, Aunt Flo?" I asked.

"Yes, I was. I swam two miles every day when I was your age."

"Two miles!" I was impressed. Two miles was a third of the way across the bay. I began to press her for details: where she swam and whom she swam with and what the world was like when she was a girl, and she began to tell me stories I had never heard before, stories about herself, about her two younger sisters (one of whom was my mother), and about her own mother and father, my grandma and grandpa. She talked about their vacations together,

129

•

first
you
have
to
row
a
little
boat

the bays and lakes they visited, and how my grandpa would sit in the sand in his one-piece bathing suit with a whistle dangling from a lanyard about his neck.

"Whenever I swam too far from shore," she said, "he would run down to the edge of the water and blow his whistle and I would have to swim back in." Her voice broke and she dropped her head, as if she was grappling with emotions she thought she had long ago laid to rest.

While she spoke I veered away from land toward the deeper, bluer waters of the bay, sailing without thinking too much about where I was heading or why. I was spirited less by the wind than by the sound of her voice spinning tales about the world from which I came, the world that nurtured me before I was born. Out there, in the center of the bay, she seemed at peace with herself; her nervous tic, so evident on land, dissolved under the benign influence of wind and wave, and I felt a closer kinship with her than at any time before.

A thin haze blew in from the ocean, hiding the mainland behind a veil of gauze. Aunt Flo grew quiet; she sat on the windward deck beside me and looked over the water toward the dim and fading shore. After a while she turned toward me and asked, "The word *atonement*—do you know what it means?"

"It means to atone for your sins. To make amends for your wrongs." I had given her a quick response, mouthing empty words, because I thought that was what she wanted to hear.

"No," she said, "it means at-one-ment—to be at one with God."

I was dumfounded by the way she broke the syllables down; I thought she was toying with words, playing a silly parlor game. But my mind wouldn't let go of what she said, and the more I thought about at-one-ment as opposed to atonement, the more her insight appealed to me. Was she trying to tell me something about myself and why I sailed? If so, her timing was perfect; she had chosen an apt moment when I was in a mood to listen to what she had to say. It was as if the blue sloop were a transforming agent, bringing out buried virtues in those who boarded her, including my guardian aunt and myself.

Years later, I discovered the concept wasn't original with Aunt Flo. Rabbis often refer to at-one-ment during Yom Kippur, the high holy Day of Atonement for Jews, and many a minister and priest has preached an at-one-ment sermon, too. But I first heard about it while sailing with her in the middle of the Great South Bay, and it stirred my thoughts as we began the long run home. I wanted to ask her what she meant by God, but I didn't dare. I was sure she would tell me about the God we beseeched in prayer, the God whose name we took in vain, the all-knowing, white-haired authoritarian figure who dwelt in the sky. But that vision didn't jibe with my own youthful view of the world and how it worked.

God, at that pagan period of my life, meant the gods of the wind, the sun, the moon, and the tides. What I sought was to enter into a state of grace with those deities, to sail until I became part of them and they part of me. My goal wasn't to harness the elements but to heed them, to attend to them closely, carefully, to ally myself with all the natural forces that ruled the world.

I began with the most willful of all divinities: the wind. As I sailed, I discovered that there wasn't one wind, but many winds, and each had its own distinctive character. There was the prevailing south-westerly which picked up speed all day as the sun warmed the land and waned at night as the earth gave up its heat. There was the gusty northwesterly, blowing mightily one minute out of some great bellows in the sky and disappearing the next, only to burst forth again more furiously than before. There was the gentle easterly, bringing with it long, sad days of drizzle and fog. And there was the relentless, raging gale from the southeast, whipping the water into a frenzy of whitecaps.

In time, I attained my goal; I became at one with the wind. I found I could tell its direction as soon as I rose in the morning and got my first clear whiff of air. I could taste its flavor on my tongue, feel its subtle pressure in my bones. If I sneezed, I knew a high, dry northerly was blowing pollen across the land; and if I slumped back on my pillow, I knew I was in the grip of a lotus southerly drifting in from

131
•
first
you
have
to
row
a
little
boat

the sea, carrying with it the unmistakable scent of tidal bog and razor clams.

I came to know the delicate sea and shorebirds, lords of the water and the air. I heard the whimbrel flying over the reeds; I saw the dowitcher feeding in the marsh mud. I saw the white egret drifting like a huge snowflake across an estuary, and the great blue heron bracing itself on spindly legs in the shallows, its bill poised for a strike. In fall, I saw migrating grebe, sheldrake and white-patched bufflehead diving expertly from the surface in pursuit of fish. And in that awesome calm before a hurricane I could count on hearing the rattling cry of the belted kingfisher up and down the brackish creeks.

During those indolent summer days aboard my sloop, I found out something fundamental about myself: I was a lazy sailor at heart. I didn't want to race, to vie with others, to see if I could make my boat fly faster than theirs; I had no yen to sail single-handedly across the ocean, no desire to circumnavigate the globe. I merely wanted to cruise this precious jewel, the Great South Bay; I wanted to ghost along with my sheets cleated and the sea swirling over the lee rail. I wanted to venture down hidden coves and harbors, skim past windswept islands, anchor off deserted beaches where I could swim or tread the sandy bottom for chowder clams.

"It is not worth the while to go round the world to count the cats in Zanzibar," Henry Thoreau wrote in *Walden*. I read those words as a man, not as a

boy, but as soon as I saw them on the printed page
I thought of those endless days of exploration aboard
my sloop, sailing a teeming body of water next door
to where I lived. Those early experiences so colored
my view that I am suspicious to this day of affluent
tourists who traipse the globe. I once met a man
who said he had visited every exotic place from
the Grand Canyon to the Great Wall, but when I
questioned him closely I discovered he hadn't seen
the songbirds in his own backyard.

What I would like to suggest to such people is
that they sit perfectly still and stare intently into a
lily pond. But that's difficult advice to give and
even more difficult to accept in a society that holds
contemplation in such low esteem. We believe in
locomotion for its own sake; we think as long as we're
flitting from place to place we're getting somewhere.
We're sprinters running mindlessly against the
clock, against ourselves, against the angel of death,
and missing the essence of our existence as we go.

What matters at this precious moment is what
has always mattered: the dailiness of life. Everything
significant is small and slow. Must we die and come
back to our tiny place on Planet Earth, as Emily
comes back in Thornton Wilder's *Our Town,* to
experience the snail's pace of love? There's no cry in
our literature more poignant, more anguished than
Emily's in that terrible moment before she returns
to her grave on the hill.

"Good-by, good-by, world. Good-by, Grover's

133
•
first
you
have
to
row
a
little
boat

Corners ... Mama and Papa. Good-by to clocks ticking ... and Mama's sunflowers. And food and coffee. And new-ironed dresses and hot baths ... and sleeping and waking up. Oh, earth, you're too wonderful for anybody to realize you. (She looks toward the stage manager and asks abruptly, through her tears) Do any human beings ever realize life while they live it?—every, every minute?"

And the stage manager replies, "No. The saints and poets, maybe—they do some."

Saints and poets, who are they if not ordinary mortals like you and me? Like them, we possess the power to paint the hour, transfigure the day. We need not wait for a church to canonize us before we become the fully conscious beings we were meant to be.

If we fail we will pay for it with our lives. I mean that literally, for the consequences of indifference to the little wonders of the world are all too plain. Even now an epidemic depression, born of boredom, spreads across the land, and we turn to violence to fill the void. Instead of watching the spider weave its web, we watch slaughter in the living room, murder in the movie house. Hopelessly addicted before we know it, we find that make-believe killings aren't enough; they no longer satisfy the gnawing hunger in our bowels. We need real mayhem, real war, real corpses to relieve the tedium that threatens to bury us alive.

In desperation we turn to fetish sporting events,

135

•

first
you
have
to
row
a
little
boat

and the trumped-up excitement smothers our pain—but only for a while. I confess I'm drawn to these spectacles—the World Series, the Stanley Cup, the Super Bowl—as much as the next man, and like the next man I have the team I root for and the team I hate. But I also know I fall into a funk once the contest ends, even if my team has won. I wander about the house, grumbling, banging closet doors, rattling dishes in the sink, facing the ennui, the emptiness of myself—and then I remember there's a better place to be.

I go down to the beach and watch how the waves curl against the shore. I study the sea fig and the sand fleas and the fiddler crabs and the peculiar upward curve of the godwit's bill. High overhead the daytime moon is climbing the eastern sky and so I know the tide is coming in. I stand in the wet sand so near the sea's edge that the incoming surf washes over my shoes. Suddenly, in the water a hundred feet away, I see a bewhiskered sea lion with his black head poked above the breakers; he is staring at me with faint amusement, as if I were the oddest creature in the world, which perhaps I am.

FIFTEEN

·

LIKE A BOAT WITHOUT A RUDDER

·

*E*arly one morning I raised my sails and tacked out of the canal, not sure where I wanted to go. When I reached open water, I decided not to cross the bay to the barrier beach, as was my custom, but to hug the mainland. I turned eastward toward the climbing sun and made a long run past familiar landmarks—

Bayberry Point, Nicoll Point, Timber Point—
with the wind behind and my sail slung out over
the side.

The heat of August was on the land and a rich,
deep foliage covered the shore. Through the leaves
I could see occasional signs of civilization: a chimney,
a gas tank, a water tower, a church steeple. I lived
there, along with thousands of others, somewhere
beyond the tree line in that suburban town. But from
the sea, under the sail of my sloop, the coast looked
sparsely settled, barely touched by human habitation
and still pristine.

It wasn't until I was skimming past the Connetquot River that I realized I had sailed a greater
distance downwind than I had intended. The onshore wind had picked up considerably and now I
had no choice except to beat against it all the way
home. I decided to jibe; it was the quickest way to
turn the boat around. I brought the wind across the
stern, and as the boom swung over the deck I lost
the ability to steer.

The tiller jiggled loosely in my hand and the boat
floundered in the breeze. I lay prone on the aft deck
and peered over the transom, trying to figure out
what had happened. After a few moments, I saw my
rudder bob up in the water about twenty feet off the
stern and float away.

Apparently, it had been yanked clear off its fasten-
ings by the force of the jibe. Unable to control the
boat, I did the only thing I could do: I lowered my

sails and let the breeze blow her broadside toward land. I looked up at the mast; it tipped one way and then the other as the oncoming waves rolled under the hull. I felt a queasiness, a sudden sweat, a dryness on the tongue. I didn't know what it was; I had never been seasick before.

139

•

first
you
have
to
row
a
little
boat

With the help of an oar, I managed to guide the sloop into the river where I threw the anchor overboard and let out enough line so that I could slip over the side near the sandy embankment and wade ashore. I made my way up a beach to a hot tar road and strolled barefoot along its grassy shoulder until I reached the main highway. After a while a teenager in a jalopy picked me up and kindly dropped me off right in front of the captain's house at the foot of Ocean Avenue.

It was midafternoon when I arrived. The captain's fishing party had already departed and he was hosing down *Nimrod*'s deck, washing scales and entrails into the creek to the raucous delight of herring gulls. I helped him pump out the bilge and fill the water tank, and when we finished those chores he turned to me and said, "So, what brings you here?"

"I lost my rudder . . . off Timber Point."

"Where is she now?"

"Anchored in the river."

"Well, I guess we better go get her."

He turned on the engine, I undid the lines, and we chugged out the waterway into the bay.

I have an old photograph of the *Nimrod* which I

look at from time to time so I can remember her graceful lines. Like so many other party boats on the bay in that era, she was originally constructed as a sailing vessel, a beamy catboat, by the renowned Crosby boat builders on Cape Cod. The captain had converted her—removed the mast, enlarged the trunk cabin, erected a canopy amidships, and installed a putt-putt engine which echoed up and down the creek, signaling his comings and goings. But her essential character remained intact; for all the changes, she was still a sailboat, and I felt at home the instant I stepped aboard.

The captain sat under the canopy, steering, and I sat on the stern beside a tattered flag, watching the wake, thinking of the event that forced me to abandon my sloop. It seemed to me that of all the mishaps that might befall a sailor, the loss of a rudder was the most distressing by far, and I lived through the incident again—as I have so many times since that day. There I was, my sails full, my sheets trim, my deck awash, and all at once my rudder parted company with my keel. One moment, I was an autonomous being; the next, a poor wretch at the mercy of wind and wave.

We found the sloop exactly as I left her, and we secured a line around the base of her mast and towed her back to Bay Shore. It was quitting time when we reached the shipyard, but Simmy, the captain, and I hauled her out anyhow to assess the damage. I was

141
·
first
you
have
to
row
a
little
boat

heartbroken when I saw her up on the ways. She looked so pitiful without her rudder, like a bird without a wing.

The next morning I was back bright and early, trailing Oscar Boehme, the yard's carpenter, as he went about his duties, hoping that by dogging his footsteps I could divert him from the task he had set for himself to the job I wanted done. But Oscar— a short, stooped man who walked with his head thrust in front of his shoulders, glancing neither to left nor right—was a singular creature who did what he had a mind to do, and instead of me pulling him onto my agenda, he pulled me onto his. He was building a sloop, half again as large as mine, deep in a shed, and when I came upon him that morning he was steaming planks in a long box and bending them to his will. One by one he fixed them to the ribs, a firm oak cage, until the ribs themselves were planked over and the human eye had no choice but to follow the lovely sheer of the hull.

I watched Oscar at work all that day, and not once did he broach the subject of my rudder. When I came back the following morning, he was still in the shed—but he wasn't working on his boat. He had made a template of my rudder and was busy cutting cedar boards on a band saw, the only power tool at his command, and evidently the only one he needed. It was a makeshift affair run from belts attached to overhead pulleys driven by a motor housed outside the shed. Whenever Oscar wanted to turn the motor on or off, he had to stroll around the side of the building and throw the switch.

I have no idea what a latter-day time and motion expert would say about the setup. I suspect he would want to put the carpenter into a tighter structure, make it "easier, simpler, quicker" for him to migrate between his band saw and its switch. But I have the uneasy feeling he would be wrong. Maybe Oscar preferred his little hikes; maybe he actually benefited from them; maybe they gave him a chance to think about what he was doing—and the periods of re-flection showed up in the quality of his work.

Oscar hummed endlessly, absently. I tried to identify his melodies; they definitely weren't the ones I heard on the hit parade. I asked Simmy about Oscar's "tunes" and he told me they were hymns. He also warned me not to ask Oscar about them— unless I wanted a sermon on how to save my soul. I took his advice and avoided the subject, but the more I watched Oscar the more certain I was that his deepest convictions were the unsung ones that resided in the nimble fingers of his hands.

From time to time Ray Muncey, the white-haired owner of the yard, would stop by the shed and stand there watching Oscar, his fingers twitching at his side. He didn't seem to be checking up on his em-ployee; he certainly never urged him to go faster or asked him what was taking him so long. After a few minutes he would leave as abruptly as he had come, without having said a word.

By noon my new rudder was finely sanded and attached to its rudder post. I crawled under the hull and applied a coat of copper antifouling paint. When I finished Simmy manned the winch and my sloop slid down the ways, gathering speed until she was afloat and then gliding like a water bird. I pulled her up to a mooring post with a boat hook, raised my sails, and tacked smartly across the creek, but as I neared the bulkhead on the far side I was seized with a sudden fear. Suppose my rudder snapped again? If I couldn't come about, I would crash stemfirst into the pier!

I pushed the tiller toward the sail; the sloop responded at once, nosing into the wind, past the wind, catching the breeze on the other side and veering across the creek. A few more tacks and I had cleared the breakwater. I'm free, I thought, free as the breeze! This was a genuine emotion for a youth whose sloop had been propped up in dry dock for the past three days. I was free to leave civilization behind with all its constraints, and that is a powerful pull for any boy reared as I was in the long shadow of Tom Sawyer and Huckleberry Finn.

But as soon as I reached open water, I found myself faced with a familiar dilemma; this freedom I cherished came with a precondition: I had to decide where I wanted to go. I could head for one of the

143

•

first
you
have
to
row
a
little
boat

islands in the bay, one of the resort communities on the barrier beach, or for my mooring post in the canal. But I wasn't drawn toward any of those. There was a place in the wind calling out to me, and it wasn't until I had left the land far in my wake that I knew for certain where it was.

I turned eastward and sailed down the wind— past Bayberry Point, Nicoll Point, Timber Point. I waited until I was off the Connetquot River, until I could see straight down its broad mouth, and then I deliberately jibed. The boom swung forcibly across the deck, over my head, but the rudder held. I trimmed my sails and began the long beat westward against wind and wave, the spray in my face, toward home.

The sun had already dropped below the rim of the land by the time I swung up to my mooring post and dropped my sails. I was thoroughly drenched and my eyelids were caked with salt, but I was so exhilarated I couldn't leave my sloop. I sat in the cockpit for a long time, watching the evening star, the rising moon, thinking about what a difference a rudder had made in the course I sailed that day.

I think about it still. I had been given a precious gift called freedom, and for a while I mistook it for the purpose of my life. I thought that because I was free to sail wherever I wanted, whenever I wanted, without seeking permission from someone else, that I possessed all I would ever need. What I discovered was that if I wanted to be free, truly free, I had to choose. There were many points on the compass rose; I had to locate the few that were meant for me.

Not any destination picked at random or reached by happenstance would do. I had to head for those that summoned me with a passion, for they were the ones that gave meaning to my life. I had to ignore the warnings of friends, the cautious ones who would tell me why I couldn't do what I wanted to do—and why. And I had to avoid the wise lies of enemies, the zealots and the despots who would try to bend me to their will.

I have a young friend, an aspiring photographer, who is an anomaly in these troubled times. He doesn't drink and he doesn't smoke and he has never messed around with drugs, and so his head is clear. "The only freedom I have is the freedom I take for myself," he said to me one day, and the audacity of his declaration took my breath away. And how does he take his freedom? He does it by carrying the purpose of his life, his camera and his tripod, with him wherever he goes.

What he practices is nothing less than revolution—a revolution of one. If every man and woman were to take the meaning of their life and pursue it passionately, they would alter the social landscape overnight. In fact, that's how lasting revolutions are made—not by the raised arm of the masses, not by the military seizure of power, not by the political coup d'etat, but by individuals asserting who they are one at a time.

145

•

first
you
have
to
row
a
little
boat

I know now there was a wayward aspect to my youth and I wouldn't disown it if I could. But there were a number of adults, none of them sailors, who were disturbed by this refusal of mine to be bound by land. On one occasion, a well-meaning friend of my uncle said to me, "You're a lucky boy. You can escape from reality whenever you choose. All you have to do is get in your boat and sail away."

The statement irritated me at the time and I didn't know why, although I do now. It was the thoughtless assumption that sailing is a childish game, a way of running out on the world. But the Great South Bay was no more an escape for me than those mythic journeys down the Mississippi were for Huck and Tom. I found a higher authority out there, a government more powerful than the one on land, a parliament of winds, a congress of tides, and I knew I had to ally myself with those forces of nature if I wanted to survive. A boy who learns he is a brother to the elements isn't likely to become estranged from them when he grows into a man.

From time to time, I go back to Bay Shore—to recall the past and see how much it has changed. Muncey's yard is long since gone, as are Muncey himself and the men who worked for him. The last time I drove down to the end of Ocean Avenue, the shed where Oscar built my rudder had been razed and replaced with a blacktop parking lot. The property, the new owners would undoubtedly say, had gone to its "highest need"—by which they would mean its most profitable use. But I would have to question their assessment, for Muncey's yard still stands in my mind as a model of what a workplace ought to be.

The environment was free and easy; the employees knew what they had to do and they did it without constant coaxing from the boss. There were no time clocks. My guess is that if Muncey had installed one, Simmy wouldn't have punched it and Oscar would have picked up his tools and gone somewhere else. They didn't work in a windowless office that looked like every other office along a dreary corridor. In fact, they had no office at all. They worked in the open air, under the sky, and they had an unobstructed view of the boats that plied the adjacent saltwater creek.

Simmy and Oscar and old man Muncey, they didn't make much money or leave behind a substantial estate, but they took their birthright; I honestly believe they did. And in so doing, they made it possible for others to take their birthright, too. That, at least, is how it seems to me when I stand in the center of the blacktop lot that was once the site of a busy shipyard. What I remember most is that one day long ago I lost my rudder, and then a superb craftsman gave it back to me, and ever since I've been at great pains not to lose it again.

147

•

first
you
have
to
row
a
little
boat

SIXTEEN

·

A BOAT IS A SHE,

A BOAT IS A HE

·

*T*here was a girl with a
willowy body and
windblown hair. She sailed
a Cape Cod knockabout
and the first time I saw her she was
tacking smartly out of the canal with her
younger brother as crew. She had a
throaty voice and I could plainly hear her
commands carrying across the water—

"Ready about! Hard-a-lee!"—and her deep whoop each time her boat crossed the wind, heeled, and sliced the other way.

My sloop was slightly larger and faster than hers, and one windy morning I pursued her out of the canal, closing the gap between us with each tack. When we reached open water, I swooped by, stealing the wind right out of her sails. Her boat lost headway and rocked from side to side, and for a while I thought she might capsize. When she finally regained control, she stood straight up beside the tiller, shook her fist at me, and let loose with a profanity. "You SOB," she shouted, "I'll get you for that, I swear I will."

I was astounded at my boldness, but I was shocked by her response. She's not a girl; she's a boy, I said to myself. Only a boy would cuss and shake a fist at me like that!—and in that moment of revelation another thought, far more disturbing, ran through my mind. If she's a boy, then she's just like me—she has the same urges and the same fears. But she wasn't a boy; she was a girl, and the siren sound of her voice followed me across the bay.

When I returned to the canal later that afternoon, I saw her knockabout at its mooring post, and I brazenly sailed up to it, turning into the wind. She was alone, kneeling on the foredeck, coiling her lines.

"I'm sorry about what happened earlier," I said.

"You ought to be," she replied.

"What can I do to make it up?"

She sat silently for a moment, and then she said, "You can take me for a sail in that lovely boat of yours—that's what you can do!"

I was taken back. I had no idea it was so easy—that all I had to do was strike up a civil conversation with a member of the opposite sex and before I knew it she would be inviting herself aboard my sloop for a sail.

"Okay," I said. "It's a deal."

She stepped lightly from the bow of her boat to the bow of mine—I barely felt the transfer of weight—and deftly back-winded the jib. The next moment, we were scooting out the canal, heading for the bay, and she was sitting beside me on the windward deck. I found out her name was Sally and that she was an accomplished sailor and had no compunctions about asserting herself.

"He handles nicely," she said. "Will you let me sail him."

"What!" I said, not sure I heard right.

"He's a lively boat," she repeated. "I'd like to sail him."

"You mean you'd like to sail her," I said. "A boat is a her."

"You're a boy," she said, "and so a boat is a her to you. But I'm a girl, and so a boat is a him to me."

I switched places with her, wondering what I had gotten myself into. I had known this girl barely ten minutes and already she was turning the natural order of my little world upside down. A boat was a

151

•

first
you
have
to
row
a
little
boat

girl—Simmy had told me that, the captain had told me that, every seafaring man I ever met had told me that, and suddenly this creature of a different persuasion was trying to tell me that a boat was a boy.

What surprised me most was that Sally sailed my sloop exactly as I sailed her, with the same feel. She knew the wind and she followed its dictates, climbing to windward as it picked up speed and falling off as soon as the peak of the mainsail started to luff, and then climbing to windward once more. That was a puzzlement; it was as if I had discovered a girl who threw a ball like a boy. Since we were different sexes, I had assumed we would have different responses to the wind and waves.

Sally and I sailed together often that summer, but try as I might there was one thing I couldn't do, and that was convince her to call a boat a she.

"He needs to have the barnacles scraped off his bottom," Sally would say.

"No she doesn't," I would reply. "Her bottom is clean."

"He would sail a lot faster."

"No she wouldn't. She sails just fine."

Late one afternoon, when we were flying home with a brisk southwesterly behind, she suddenly blurted out in her irresistible way, "Let's race him."

"I don't like to race," I replied.

"Just once," she persisted. "I bet we can win." She

153

·

first
you
have
to
row
a
little
boat

pointed out that a local yacht club was sponsoring a handicap race, open to boats of all classes, shapes, and sizes.

"Who would be the skipper?" I asked. I didn't think she would crew for me, and I certainly wasn't going to crew for her—I had heard the way she bossed her brother around—but she had the answer to that question, too.

"We have to go around the course twice," she said. "You sail her the first time around and I'll sail him the second time around. Don't you see—that way we can't lose."

Her enthusiasm was contagious and so I agreed, saying to myself, I will race this one time, and then I will never race again.

We went out on the roughest days and practiced tacking and jibing. I would tend the sheets while she handled the helm and then we would switch places. One day I came aboard with an old spinnaker I had never used, and we flew it on a downwind leg and it pulled me overboard. She came about and fished me out and we tried again, taking turns until we could raise and lower the huge balloon of a sail without going for a swim.

We sailed out early on the day of the race and headed for the committee boat, bedecked with flying pennants, a mile offshore. I had never seen so many sails dipping and soaring in the same place, vying for the same wind at the same time. A gun went off, startling us both, and five seconds later we crossed the starting line—not in the best position but not in the worst.

Most of the boats were jockeying at the windward end of the line, which was the ideal place to be. But we elected to avoid the heavy traffic and crossed more to leeward where the wind was free. It was a calculated risk; we would have some distance to make up over the course of the race, but unlike the other boats, which were huddled together, blocking each other's wind, trying to get out of each other's way, we were moving at top speed from the moment we hit the starting line.

I settled low on the lee side of the sloop, the way the captain taught me, with the tiller over my shoulder, guiding it gently between my forefinger and thumb. I didn't see the other boats on that first windward leg; I wasn't aware of the passage of time. Every now and then, Sally would tell me we were "catching up, catching up," but I didn't care. I was exhilarated not by the race but by the mystical link between myself and the sloop as she sliced through the sea. I was sailing now with a sense of grace I had never known before.

When we completed three legs of the triangular course, I turned the tiller over to Sally and looked over the water for the first time. The larger, swifter sloops were well ahead of us and the smaller, slower ones were well behind, but that didn't matter because the winning sloop would not necessarily be the first

155

•

first
you
have
to
row
a
little
boat

to cross the finish line. We weren't competing against all those other boats; we were competing against the clock, which is just another way of saying we were competing against ourselves.

Sally sailed the three legs exactly as I had, making the most of the freshening breeze—heading up, falling off, and heading up again, never sacrificing vital momentum, always aware of hull speed. As she deftly guided the sloop, I felt as if we were joined by our common purpose, sharing the same place at the same precious moment, and the unfortunate part was that I was too young to know how far I would have to sail before I found such companionship again.

We cruised about until the last boat crossed the finish line, and then we tied up at the yacht club dock and milled about with the other sailors, waiting for the race committee to post the results. Sally was excited, and so was I, even though I acted as if I didn't care. "I think we did well," she kept saying, "I think we did real well," and I kept shrugging my shoulders and saying, "I don't know. We'll have to wait and see, won't we? We'll have to wait and see."

At last the commodore appeared, adorned in a fancy cap with gold braiding, a navy blue blazer with brass buttons and an insignia on the chest, and white duck pants. He held a piece of paper in one hand and a megaphone in the other, and he began to announce the boats with the best corrected time. We weren't first; that honor belonged to a swift *R* class racing sloop that had won the event several years in a row. And we weren't second; an upstart Narrasketuck, which must have flown around the course, claimed that distinction. We were about to abandon all hope when the voice coming over the megaphone revealed that we were third.

It wasn't the trophy we sought, but it was good enough; in fact, it was better than good enough, and Sally and I hugged each other and danced around the dock. We had come out of nowhere, a couple of tyros in a blue sloop. Of the thirty or so boats entered in the regatta, we had outsailed all but two.

In the flush of victory it was hard to know why we did as well as we did—or even care. But I believe the answer lies not so much in practical seamanship as in the give and take between a boy and a girl. Ours was an unlikely liaison, one that began in disrespect. I had stolen the wind out of her sails; she had called me an ugly name; and from that shaky premise a friendship grew.

It was the sloop herself, himself, who taught us how to behave. Through sailing together, we each learned things about each other we didn't know before. As an inexperienced sailor, I tried to dominate my boat, to drive her here and force her there, to make her submissive to my will. But she convinced me quickly that there were some things she would do and some things she wouldn't, and if I wanted the pleasure of her company I had better learn the difference between the two.

157

•

f i r s t
y o u
h a v e
t o
r o w
a
l i t t l e
b o a t

What lessons Sally learned I can't say for sure, but I suspect they can be found in the ample connotations of the pronoun *he*. Perhaps to her a sloop was a powerful hull thrusting through swelling seas—or an artful machine that engaged the breeze. If so, she learned not to condemn those traits but to hold them in high esteem.

I was too innocent to know it then, but I know it now: A boat is an androgynous being, part male, part female. It takes the virtues of each sex and blends them in ways that make it impossible to tell which belong to the woman and which to the man. What I gathered from my sloop wasn't its masculinity but its womanhood; what Sally gathered wasn't its femininity but its manliness.

The world struggles with this hidden knowledge, refusing to acknowledge that men are women and women are men. And so we stereotype each other, and end up stereotyping ourselves. Harassment begins at that point where the man browbeats the woman within him and the woman stomps all over her inner man. I like to think Sally and I were lucky; for one brief moment we sailed out of our conventional identities, and that made us far more formidable contenders than if we had competed as a boy and a girl.

I kept my word; I never raced again, and yet I confess I often lie awake at night and think about the day Sally and I took turns around a triangular course and came in third. The wind is light at first and then it gathers force as the sun climbs the sky and warms the land. We are soaring on the thermals of a summer day, drawing our strength from the dual nature of the sloop we sail.

I would like to say something romantic occurred between Sally and me, but it wouldn't be true. We became friends—went to a few movies and a school dance—but that winter she moved with her family to another town. We wrote for a while and then, ages ago, drifted our separate ways. But I would like to see her again someday, if only to tell her, after all these years, that I know she was right. A boat can be a she, and a boat can be a he. There's only one thing a boat can't be, and that's an it.

SEVENTEEN
·
TRUE AND APPARENT WIND
·

*W*hat's the difference between true wind and apparent wind?" a would-be friend named Carlton Oldfield asked me one day. He wasn't looking for information; he already knew the answer. He was trying to stump me, which he did.

"I don't know," I replied, and he

159

proceeded to tell me, going into detail about such abstruse subjects as Bernoulli's principle and the theory of flight. He didn't own a boat; as far as I knew, he had never in his life left terra firma, but he had been checking sailing texts out of the public library and then accosting me with his knowledge.

"What's the difference between the leech and luff on a sail?" he asked.

I knew one was the inner edge that ran along the mast and the other was the outer edge that formed the hypotenuse of the triangle, but I could never keep straight which was which.

"Carlton," I said, "I don't know. . . ." I was about to add that I really didn't care, but he delved so quickly into his explanation that I didn't get a chance.

"Tell me," he asked another time, "what's the best angle to rake a mast?"

"I don't worry about the rake of my mast," I replied, not trying to conceal my exasperation.

"You should analyze the rake of your mast," he said. "You might gain as much as a degree to windward if you angle it a little more toward the stern."

After that encounter, I tried to avoid Carlton, but he always managed to track me down. When I went to my sloop to raise her sails, I would find him sitting on the bulkhead, his legs dangling over the edge, waiting for me. I knew he wanted me to invite him for a sail, but I never did. I would cast off, leaving him standing on the shore with a forlorn look on his face.

161

•

first
you
have
to
row
a
little
boat

One morning he intercepted me before I could board my boat.

"Guess what?" he said.

"I can't imagine," I replied.

"I got a boat."

The news surprised me. I was certain Carlton wanted to study boats, not sail them.

"What kind?" I asked.

"A fiberglass daysailer."

Fiberglass boats were new on the market. I had never sailed one but had a built-in prejudice against them. The mere idea of building a boat by embedding strands of glass in plastic struck me as unnatural. Boats were supposed to be made of wood.

Carlton looked at me expectantly. I'm sure he wanted me to respond enthusiastically to his announcement. When I didn't, he said, "What's the matter with fiberglass? My father says fiberglass boats will be around long after wooden ones have rotted away."

How could I argue against his father? For all I knew, he might be right; it was a terrible thought, but maybe the wood hull was doomed.

"When did you get the boat?" I asked.

"Three weeks ago."

"So how does it sail?"

After a hesitation, he said, "I don't know. I haven't sailed it yet."

"You mean you've had this fiberglass boat of yours for three weeks and you haven't sailed it yet!"

"My father says I have to get someone to go out with me. Someone with experience."

I wasn't about to volunteer. If Carlton wanted me to show him how to handle his boat, he was going to have to ask. But I felt vindicated. Here was this know-it-all pretending to be a sailor and he couldn't get out of the harbor without my help.

"I was thinking . . . maybe you'd go out with me."

He was a pest, a regular pest, and I waited a long time before I replied, even though I knew that I would agree. In part, I was curious about this glass sloop of his and I wanted to see for myself how she sailed, but mostly I wanted to get back at Carlton—to lord it over him as he had lorded it over me.

"All right," I said. "But not today."

"When?"

"Tomorrow."

"Good. My chauffeur will pick you up at ten."

My chauffeur will pick you up at ten! I couldn't quite comprehend what he had said, and the sentence kept rumbling through my head. *My chauffeur will pick you up at ten!* What the devil did he mean? It wasn't until a long black Cadillac pulled up in front of my house the next morning that I fully understood. He meant his chauffeur was going to pick me up at ten.

Carlton was sitting in the backseat, looking as gloomy as the day I sailed away and left him standing on the dock. I knew he was rich, but I didn't know how rich until we turned down a long bluestone driveway that led to an imposing Tudor mansion which overlooked the bay. The dwelling looked more like a fortress than a house, and I realized with a shock that I had sailed by it many times, wondering what sort of people lived inside.

The chauffeur dropped us off at the back of the property, which bordered a deeply dredged saltwater creek. The first thing I saw was a cabin cruiser, at least forty feet long, tied up beside the bulkhead, with a uniformed captain polishing its brasswork. A half dozen adults were gathered around a table in the cockpit, talking and laughing, playing cards.

"Is that your boat?" I asked Carlton, meaning, Does that boat belong to your family?

"Oh no," he replied, "that boat belongs to my father."

"Where's your boat?"

"Over there," he said, pointing to a boat house.

That's great, I thought. Putting a boat in a house made as much sense to me as putting a sweater on a dog.

I pulled her out of the shed and tied her to a cleat at the end of a dock, nose into the wind, and took a long look at her one-piece molded hull. She was about twenty feet long and had surprisingly pleasing lines, but, other than the fact that she had a centerboard instead of a keel, it was hard for me tell how she might differ from my boat under sail.

I dumped the sails out of a canvas bag and told Carlton to attach the jib to the forestay while I

163

•

first
you
have
to
row
a
little
boat

slid the mainsail onto the boom and mast. When I finished I glanced toward the yacht and saw a tall, lean man climb over the side and walk toward us across the manicured lawn, holding a highball glass in one hand. He moved slowly, deliberately, as if he knew exactly where he was going and was in no particular hurry to get there.

As he neared I could see that he was wearing a blue silk shirt tucked into white duck pants and that his gray hair was meticulously combed behind his ears. His skin was as smooth as his shirt, but his eyes were sunken. It wasn't until he had reached the edge of the bulkhead that Carlton realized the man was there—and he immediately became confused.

"Oh—this is my father," he said, and then, pointing at me, added, "And this is . . ." But he was so distracted, he couldn't remember my name. It didn't make any difference; it was plain his father didn't care.

He merely looked down at me, without seeing me, and said, "Carlton and I are so pleased that you have consented to teach him how to sail." And before I could utter a word in response, he turned and walked back to his yacht at the same deliberate pace. I had never had an adult speak to me like that before. I had been scolded, complimented, warned, and praised, but I had never been talked to as if I wasn't there.

I was embarrassed, not for myself but for Carlton, and when I turned toward him I saw he was fumbling

with the jib halyard, trying to attach it to the head
of the sail, and his cheeks were burning red. The
task was simple, but he couldn't do it—he was too
upset. His father's phrasing was subtle, but his inten-
tion was clear; he wanted to put down his son in
front of his friend—and he had succeeded without
exerting much effort at all.

A few minutes later, I heard the roar of the twin
screws that powered the yacht. I saw the captain
gather in the bow lines and deftly turn the boat on
its axis in the center of the creek and head toward
the bay. The captain gunned the engine, raising a
huge wake, and we had to fend off as best we could
to keep the sloop from crashing against the dock.
As the powerboat swept by, I saw Carlton's father
sprawled on a plush cushion in the cockpit, his face
lifted toward the sun.

I suppose this encounter with the father should
have softened me toward the son, but it didn't—
mainly because it seemed to make Carlton even
more overbearing than before. He insisted on taking
the tiller and tacking out of the creek while I tended
the jib sheets, but he made such a mess of it—losing
headway each time we came about—that he finally
agreed to turn the helm over to me. As we zigzagged
toward the bay, I tried to tell him when to let out
the jib on one side and trim it on the other, but his
timing was poor; it was as if he had no idea where
the wind was in relation to the sails.

I sailed up to a red nun a half mile offshore and

165

•

first
you
have
to
row
a
little
boat

turned the helm over to him, and he steered a yawing course, jerking the tiller back and forth, letting the mainsail out too far and then trimming it in too close. After losing headway, he would shout, "Ready about—hard-a-lee!" for no good reason and then try to bring the bow of the boat across the eye of the wind. Without momentum, the sloop would get caught "in irons" and drift backward, and he would start to jiggle the tiller mindlessly in a futile attempt to get her moving again.

After several episodes like that, I began to lose my patience. "Trim the mainsail tight!" I said. "Let her heel—and then come about!" He listened too well. He trimmed the sheet as far as it would go and when we were tilted way over he slammed the tiller across the cockpit as hard as he could. The boat shot across the wind, came to a dead halt, and sat there like a tenpin about to be struck by a bowling ball.

"Let out the sail! Let out the sail!" I shouted, but my warning came too late. The gusting wind smacked the tightly trimmed sail with such force that it knocked the boat down. The sail hit the water; the sloop tried to rise again, like a wounded bird, but the sheer weight of the wet canvas pulled her back down. The bay poured over the deck into the cockpit and the boat flopped over on her side, keel exposed and mast submerged.

I clambered toward the bow, perfectly dry, but Carlton was in the water, still clinging to the main-

sheet as if it were a lifeline, huffing and puffing, the
waves washing over his head.

"Can you swim! Can you swim!" I asked. It wasn't
so much a question as a plea.

"No," he replied, and I thought, My God, he's
going to drown!

I knelt on the gunwale and frantically waved my
arms, hoping to attract the attention of a passing
boat, and then I saw a cabin cruiser bearing down
on us. It was Carlton's father's yacht.

A minute later, we were both aboard the powerboat. Carlton was inside a blanket, soaked to the
bone and shivering, but somehow I had escaped
without getting my sneakers wet. Mr. Oldfield was
leaning against the cabin, a pair of binoculars dangling about his neck. I had to assume he had witnessed our entire mishap from afar.

"Well, well," he said at last, "I'm not surprised;
I'm not surprised at all. I suppose now you'll catch
your death of cold."

"It wasn't my fault," Carlton blurted out, pointing
an accusing finger at me. "He kept telling me to trim
the sail, trim the sail! If he hadn't kept telling me to
trim the sail, we wouldn't have tipped over!" But by
then Mr. Oldfield was gazing far out over the water,
as if he couldn't possibly permit himself to be bothered any further by the trouble we had caused.

After that Carlton and I steered clear of each
other, although I often saw his fiberglass daysailer

167

•

first
you
have
to
row
a
little
boat

on the bay. I noticed that he had learned to come about without capsizing; but I also noticed that whenever he sailed, his father's yacht was never far away. I had this image of Mr. Oldfield aboard his cabin cruiser, watching his son through his field glasses—waiting for him to do something wrong. And I had a mirror image of Carlton trying so hard to win his father's approval that he never really learned to sail.

With the passage of time, Mr. Oldfield's prediction turned out to be true; boats with fiberglass hulls came to dominate the bay, while those with wood hulls rotted away. The newer boats had their advantages; they were lighter, stronger, easier to maintain, and they could be molded into almost any shape conceived by man. But my bias remained, and it was a long time before I could bring myself to step aboard a boat with a plastic hull again.

Then one day a friend who had bought a fiberglass sloop on the Connecticut shore asked me to help him sail it around to the Great South Bay. He was a good companion and a superb sailor, and I was surprised at how smoothly the boat handled under his command. We cut across Block Island Sound, through Plum Gut, and while we were skimming along the placid waters of Peconic Bay I told him about Carlton Oldfield and the day we tipped over his fiberglass boat.

He laughed when I finished; it is a humorous story, I suppose. But in the telling of it, I realized

169
.
first
you
have
to
row
a
little
boat

exactly what it was about my miserable experience with Carlton that irked me so. It wasn't that his boat defied tradition—that it was made of an artificial rather than a natural material. It wasn't that he was an imperious skipper and a royal bore. It wasn't even that he was a "plumber"—the worst epithet one sailor could call another when I was a boy.

It was that Carlton was trying to present the world with an image of himself that was patently false. He thought that if he was seen at the helm of a boat made of glass and resin, instead of cedar and oak, he would be deemed a better sailor than he really was. He couldn't understand that the people whose esteem he so desperately desired were judging him not by the kind of boat he owned but by the way he sailed.

Yet I must confess that a question Carlton raised, one I couldn't answer, continued to nag at me for a long time. Then one day, long after we capsized, I ran into my high school physics teacher, a sometime sailor, and asked him if he had ever heard of Bernoulli's principle. He told me it was a law that had to do with fluids in motion—the faster they flow the lower the pressure. Air moves faster across the top of a wing than the bottom; that's what gives a plane its lift. The same idea also applies to a sloop. It is air curving rapidly behind the mainsail that gave my boat its forward thrust.

"There's true wind," he said, "which is the wind we feel when the boat is at anchor or in its berth.

And there's apparent wind, which is a combination of true wind and the wind the boat creates as it surges through the sea. The able sailor sails the apparent wind."

That was something I didn't know before. He was an authentic teacher and so I learned from him.

I don't know what became of Carlton, but I have come across so many people like him in my lifetime that I have to believe he's no different as a man than he was as a boy. I believe he still carries his father's voice around in his head and hears it wherever he goes. I believe he doesn't do what he wants to do but what he thinks his father would like him to do, and so the never-ending quest for parental approval continues to govern his behavior, as if his father were watching his every move from the grave.

Except the voice no longer belongs to his father alone; I believe it belongs to his friends, his neighbors, his boss, his wife—yes, even his children—who form a collective board of review. I believe he thinks they are judging him, always judging him, and so he is constantly trying to prove that he is worthy of their admiration and love. He does all the right things: He lives in a fashionable house in an exclusive neighborhood; he goes to church every Sunday, impeccably dressed in the most expensive clothes; and he makes sure his children go to the best schools.

He owns a boat, of course—larger, sleeker, faster than the one we capsized—but he's still unsure of himself when he takes the helm and he has trouble keeping track of the wind. He luffs, falls off, and luffs again—searching, endlessly searching but never finding the one true place that feels like home.

I feel sorry for Carlton Oldfield, and if I were to meet him again I know what I would like to say: "Let him go, let him go!" I know fathers are supposed to let go of sons, mothers of daughters, but I also know that it rarely happens that way. Parents cling to their children beyond all enduring, as if they have an absolute right to control their lives from the day they're born. And so the onus passes from generation to generation until a child appears with the innate power to break the bind. That is the way of all flesh.

171

•

first
you
have
to
row
a
little
boat

EIGHTEEN

·

IN PRAISE OF

SAILING MASTERS

·

One summer day, I was sitting on the deck of a friend's cottage that overlooks one of those lovely kettle ponds that dot Cape Cod. A fluky breeze was blowing out of the north, and I was trying hard not to watch my teenage son, who had never sailed before, maneuver a tiny Sunfish in the middle of the lake. His sail was hoisted two-thirds of the way up the mast, so the boom hung low and narrowly missed his head every time he came about or accidentally jibed, which he often did.

I was sure he would enjoy himself more if he raised his sail to the top of the mast, but I was reluctant to tell him so. "Let him learn for himself; let him learn for himself!" I kept repeating under my breath. It was sound advice; it was also impossible to follow. My eyes kept drifting from the book I was reading to the Sunfish skimming erratically across the pond.

That sagging sail of his struck me as an indiscretion, a social blunder; I didn't want a son of mine cruising about in such an unseemly manner. When I couldn't bear the sight of it any longer, I climbed down a flight of wooden steps and waded knee-deep into the water, where I stood amid a bunch of lily pads, waving my arms, trying to catch his attention. He finally saw me and headed toward shore, turning the wrong way and jibing again. Luckily, the wind was light and he averted disaster.

When he was within earshot, I made a hand-over-hand motion, as if I was pulling downward on the main halyard, and shouted, "Raise your sail up higher! The boat will go much better!"

"Oh, Pop," he said, "why don't you leave me alone! I'm just trying to have some fun!" And he yanked the tiller, jibing the boat again, and headed for the opposite shore, with the boom dragging across the deck.

175
·
first
you
have
to
row
a
little
boat

I was miffed and hurt, as upset with myself as I was with him. I had wanted to pass some measure of myself on to my son; it was a reaching out, an attempt to say, Here's what I once learned; I offer it as a gift from the boy in me to the boy in you. My son had rejected what I had to tell him, the lessons I had so painstakingly gathered in my sailing youth.

I picked up my book and tried to read, but I couldn't concentrate. I laid the book on my lap, lifted my head, and closed my eyes; I could feel the bright ball of sun burning through my lids. A buried memory from another land drifted through my mind . . .

Father and son meet on the banks of a river that flows into eternity. The son reviles and vilifies the old man who doesn't deign to reply. The father merely sits silently and contemplates the river which runs ceaselessly by his side. It is the river beyond insight, beyond knowledge, beyond pride; it is the river that flows beyond the self that constantly strives to explain. Siddhartha now knows what he knows; he has reached a state of being where he no

longer feels the need to justify himself to
his son. . . .

I had read that timeless scene from the book by
Herman Hesse long before my son was born, and
now it rose from some silent place within myself
and spoke to me once more, forcing me to consider
the way I behaved. "Why must I wade into the pond
and stand there stupidly waving my arms? Why
must I tell my son he would be better off if he raised
his sail higher up the mast?" I tried to banish the
incident from my mind, but I was not Siddhartha
and the image of the sagging sail remained with me
through the long afternoon.

But my son is a sensitive son, and that evening,
while dining at a fish house, he discreetly raised the
subject of sailing, asking me to explain the difference
between a tack and a jibe. I could tell by the tone of
his voice that he knew he had wounded me, that he
was trying to make amends, and so I let go of my
hurt and constructed a reply. Using a fork as a
sailboat, I pretended the wind was blowing across
the table from him toward me, and I brought the
bow of the fork across the wind for a tack and the
stern of the fork across for a jibe.

The demonstration served its purpose; it momentarily cleared the air. But later that evening, while
sitting alone on the deck above the darkening pond,
I was oppressed again by the vision of the sagging
sail. The unspoken words welled up within me and

I conducted an imaginary conversation with my son, telling him quietly and gently what I longed to tell him, passing on the legacy of what I knew.

177

•

first
you
have
to
row
a
little
boat

First find the fickle wind. Ask yourself where it's coming from and what it's doing now that it has never done before. Determine which is the lee side of the lake, for that is the protected place where the wind begins, the place of greatest calm. Watch the tops of the trees that rim the lake; observe the leaves, the ripples on the surface of the water, the movement of the other boats. They will let you know where the breeze appears and where it vanishes as it blows from shore to shore.

Make sure that the sheets are free and not tangled or secured, so the boat won't start sailing in circles around her mooring when you raise the sail. Hoist the sail, raising it as high up the mast as it will go, and let it flutter in the breeze. Drop the centerboard, check the rudder to make sure it's firmly fixed, and then step back and stare at the boat until she is so indelibly imprinted in your mind that you can see her plainly with your eyes closed.

Think of how the boat will behave when she's under way, how she will dip and soar. Listen to the sound of the wind in the rigging, the gentle slurping of the hull. Grasp the tiller, feel the subtle pressure of it in your hand—how you move it toward the sail or away from the sail to change your angle to the wind.

Tack without tacking, jibe without jibing; shift

your weight without moving as the boat heels. Wait until you know for certain that your boat is not an object outside yourself, but an aspect of yourself, an extension of who you are. When you reach that moment where you and the boat and the wind are at one with one another, you are ready to sail.

It was a sermon with a serious flaw; it was delivered to the night air—but given the conflicts that so often arise between parents and children I thought perhaps it was better that way. If my son were present, he would have done exactly what I would have done at the same age: fidgeted in his seat, rolled his eyes, and hoped that the lecture wouldn't last too long. He needed someone to teach him to sail, but as much as I wanted to be his mentor I knew it couldn't be me.

I sat there for a long time, watching the surrounding sand hills merge with the sky. I knew this pond, knew it well. It had been formed when the last glacier passed this way about ten thousand years ago. As it retreated, it left behind a giant chunk of ice that melted slowly, leaving a symmetrical depression in the land. In time, underground springs filled the bowl, creating a freshwater lake within a mile of the pounding sea.

The full moon rose over the rim of the dunes and cast a shimmering light across the pond. After a while, I envisioned a Sunfish with a sagging sail, and

179

•

first
you
have
to
row
a
little
boat

in that vision I saw my son pull down on the halyard, raising the sail to the top of the mast, and then I saw the sailboat skim the pond on the errant breeze. He sailed out of his own knowing without any direction from me. In that elusive moment I remembered what I had felt as a boy and forgotten as a man, and I knew I had to set my son free so he might find his masters—as I had found mine.

As a youth, I had regarded the loss of my parents as the central tragedy of my life. But as I grew older, I began to see that I had certain advantages over my friends, who had no choice except to model themselves after the parents they had. For a few that worked out, but for most it didn't, and many had to rebel before they could discover who they were. But I had no such impediment in my way. I could choose my models wherever I found them, and I found them everywhere. I didn't have to limit myself to one father and one mother; I could pick and reject as many as I wanted as I went along—and that's what I did.

I picked Capt. Harrison Watts, who taught me how to row a little boat and how to climb the wind. I picked Ed Doubrava, who showed me the shortcuts across the shoals and flats and found my first sailboat, a makeshift duck blind, buried in the cattails. I picked Simmy Baker, who taught me how to splice a rope and persuaded me to keep my centerboard lowered at all times.

These men were my masters—and I had chosen them; they hadn't chosen me. They didn't impose themselves by offering gratuitous advice. If they saw a novice floundering in the wind, they didn't rush up and tell him how to trim his sails. But if that same novice approached them later on and sought their counsel, neither did they turn their backs.

Taciturn? To be sure—that's how baymen were when I was a youth. But they were also men of character who didn't hoard their knowhow but passed on freely what they knew to any sailor who had sense enough to ask.

I sat on the deck overlooking the pond for a long time with these thoughts racing through my mind. The moon, which had risen when the sun had set, had now climbed halfway across the sky. I rose stiffly from my Adirondack chair, checked my son, who was fast asleep, and collapsed on a bed in the room next door.

When I awoke, a faint wind was blowing through my window and the light of dawn was in the eastern sky. I climbed down the wooden steps and waded out to the Sunfish, hoisting her sail as high as it would go. I attached the rudder, dropped the center-board, and stood quietly in the water, listening to the luffing of the sail. When I was ready, I clambered aboard and sailed the mile across the pond and back again.

I returned with the wind behind, and when I

reached the shallows I raised the board and beached the boat, skimming up the sandy shore. I was about to lower the sail when I saw my son sitting on a nearby log, intently watching me.

"Do you want to take her out?" I asked.

"Why not," he replied.

He pulled the Sunfish to its mooring and let her nose into the wind. Slowly, hand over hand, he hoisted the sail until he couldn't hoist it any higher. He stood for a few minutes, staring at the boat, and then he pushed her off and slipped aboard. The sail caught the wind; the boat heeled sharply and veered across the glassy surface of the pond. I went to the cottage and sat on the deck, sipping coffee and watching my son, astounded at how much he had learned about sailing in so short a time.

All that happened long ago, but I have finally figured out what it means. Everyone needs a master—my experience with a Sunfish on a Cape Cod kettle pond convinces me that's true. But not any master will do. We don't need critics to impress us with their knowledge, and we don't need lecturers to talk to us as if we weren't there. We don't need people who hector us, badger us, teach us by rote, for they teach nothing at all. What we do need is someone who can show us how to tie a clove hitch or set a whisker pole.

Life is an apprenticeship; I didn't know that when I first raised a sail, but I know it now. We are

181
·
first
you
have
to
row
a
little
boat

standing on the shoulders of giants who helped de-
scribe the character of our universe long before we
came along. We may like to think we are born
knowing all we need to know and that what we don't
know will come to us through happenstance. But if
we want to learn, truly want to learn, we must break
through the protective veneer of false pride and
allow the masters of the past and present to enter
our lives.

We need to find those special people who contain
the lore of the race and can pass on to us what we
yearn to know. They may be individuals we meet
personally in the classroom or the shipyard or the
office down the hall. Or they may be individuals we
never meet and never can meet because they belong
to another age—although we know them well by
the works they left behind.

If we want to write, we need a master who speaks
to us in a voice that bears a kinship to our own.
Early in life I chose Henry Thoreau and Willa Cather
and Leo Tolstoy. If we want to paint, we need a
master whose vision of light, form, and color appeals
to our inner eye. If we want to compose, we need a
master whose music touches our soul. If we want to
sail, we need a master who knows right down to his
fingertips the subtle balance among wind and sea
and sail.

My son never sailed again; he had other things to
do, other places to go, and he didn't have the same
compulsion about a sloop in the wind that governed

me. He went on to be an expert fisherman and a superb cabinetmaker, and for those endeavors he found his own masters, the ones who spoke to him. By then I had enough sense to give him my blessing and get out of his way.

183

•

first
you
have
to
row
a
little
boat

NINETEEN

·

WHEN TO SELL A SLOOP

·

I sailed the blue sloop through high school, through college, through the early years of my marriage, and she never once shipped water through her hull. But one morning after a heavy rain, I checked her and saw that she was sitting below her waterline. I stepped aboard and tasted the water in the bilge; it had a slightly salty flavor. I had better keep a close eye on her, I told myself as I pumped her out, but I had trouble heeding my own warning.

I was well into my twenties at the time. I was working as a reporter on a local newspaper, a job that kept me under constant deadline pressure, and the birth of my first child was days away. A gory murder, a political fracas, a school board showdown, and my wife's condition occupied my thoughts, pushing the leaky sloop into the back of my mind.

Check the boat, check the boat!—but as soon as those words entered my head another crisis intervened.

Late one afternoon, while sitting at my typewriter, I got the expected phone call. I raced home, took my wife to the hospital, raced back to the news office to finish the story, and then raced back to the hospital again. The baby, I discovered, wasn't exactly in a hurry to be born; my wife's labor pains had stopped as suddenly as they started—and then they started, stopped, and started again.

After two nerve-racking days, she delivered a boy at two o'clock in the morning. I went home, fell into a fitful sleep, and woke up early to the incessant ringing of the phone. I grabbed the receiver, expecting to hear my doctor's voice, or possibly my wife's, but it was neither of those. It was the harbormaster and he was addressing me in funereal tones.

187
•
first
you
have
to
row
a
little
boat

"I hate to be the one to tell you this," he said, "but your boat sank."

"What!"

"Sank! Sank! She's sitting on the bottom. The only thing above water is the mast."

I threw on some clothes, drove to the canal, and stood on the edge of the bulkhead, staring at the saddest sight in the world. The harbormaster had described the scene accurately; the blue sloop was totally submerged, her heavy wooden mast poking through the surface of the water and tilted toward the sky, and I was filled with guilt, as if I had committed a heinous crime.

On the way to the hospital, I stopped at the shipyard and tried to explain to old man Muncey what had happened.

"My wife had a baby last night," I said, "and my boat sank."

"My congratulations and condolences," he said, succinctly summing up my plight.

For a long time I thought those two events—the sinking of my boat and the birth of my son—were mere coincidence, but I no longer believe that's so. In fact, I'm not sure I believe in coincidence at all. When two seemingly unrelated events occur simultaneously, we at least owe it to ourselves to question why. One phase of my life was coming to a close and another was about to begin. That much should have been clear. But at that moment I was more invested in my submerged sloop than in my newborn son.

Muncey raised the boat, towed her around to the yard, and hauled her up on the ways. The water drained out through the garboard seam, the place where the wood hull meets the keel. Oscar Boehme ripped out the rotting plank and fashioned a new one. A week later, the boat was back in the water and the baby was home in his crib—and I had two whopping bills, one from the hospital and the other from the shipyard.

When I was younger, my uncle helped pay for the upkeep of the sloop, but now the full burden fell on me. Mooring fees, winter storage, maintenance, repairs: I had to lay out the money for those items myself. The cost kept increasing every year—and so did my family: another son, a daughter, eventually a second daughter, and a house with a mortgage big enough to accommodate us all.

I sailed whenever I could, which wasn't often, leaving my family back on shore. If I had been an accountant, I would have balked at the unit cost of each voyage across the bay. I knew I was no longer getting my money's worth out of my boat, but I wasn't a bookkeeper and I refused to cost-account each tack and jibe. But there is one thing about a checkbook; it doesn't lie.

On one of my infrequent ventures into the bay, I noticed my mainsail was badly frayed along a batten seam. And then one day in a high wind, it split completely apart. I took it to a sailmaker who told me it was futile to try to repair it. He said I needed a new sail—nothing but a new sail would do, and while I was at it I should also invest in a jib. I knew he was right; I also knew I didn't have seven hundred dollars in my account, so I took out a bank loan. The new sails were well made and fit perfectly, improving the upwind efficiency of my sloop, but whenever I raised them I was reminded of the monthly payment, which was usually past due.

My wife and I talked about selling the boat, but each time the subject came up I made the same resolve. "I will keep the boat, come what may," I said. "Someday the kids will be old enough to sail, and then we'll be glad we hung on to it—you'll see!"

After my second son was born, I found a job on the editorial staff of a magazine in Manhattan, joining the ranks of commuters who caught the 7:10 train to work every morning and the 6:07 train home every night. The twelve-hour workdays, including the trips from home to office and back again, left me exhausted. When the weekend came, I still wanted to sail, but I found it was easier to pack my kids into the backseat of my car than the small cockpit of my boat, and so I didn't sail at all.

As I rode the commuter express, I would gaze out the window at the Long Island landscape, which was undergoing rapid change. In the wake of World

189

•

first
you
have
to
row
a
little
boat

War II, the developers had moved in and bought up the farms and cleared the woods, replacing corn, potatoes, oak, and scrub pine with mile upon square mile of tract homes. It was a profitable enterprise; the land was flat. All they had to do was subdivide it and sink their foundations in the sand.

In the Town of Islip, the geopolitical unit where I lived and began my reporting career, the population jumped from 15,000 to 150,000 in a few years. There were no sewer systems; the cesspools and septic tanks seeped into the rivers and creeks that flowed into the bay. My children couldn't wade into the shallows and tread for cherrystones and chowder clams the way I did when I was their age.

I should get out of here, go someplace else, I would say to myself. I felt an acute sense of loss on those long, sorrowful rides; the rural world I knew as a boy was being taken from me, and there was nothing I could do. But moving meant selling my boat, and that was something I wasn't ready to do.

There's an aspect to materialism that has to do with possession for its own sake, as if the goods we own are a measure of who we are. But there's another aspect that has to do with attachment to objects themselves long after they have ceased to serve their original purpose in our lives. I know a couple who can barely abide each other, yet they find it impossible to separate because neither can bear the thought of leaving the Victorian house in which they dwell. They aren't married to each other; they're married to double-hung windows and oak doorjambs and the varnished banister on the stairs.

It's a sad predicament, and yet I can understand how difficult it is to break the bond with those physical things that tie us to our past. I was wedded to my sloop; she was a part of me, but circumstances had transformed her from an asset into an encumbrance. And yet I believed I would lose the essence of myself, my identity as a sailor, if I let her go.

I was wrong, of course; the value of my sloop wasn't in her wood hull, her lead keel, her canvas sails. Her value was in the lessons she taught me as I grew from a boy into a man, and those lessons would remain with me long after she was gone. "Be with what is so that what is to be may become," wrote Sören Kierkegaard. I'm not now nor was I ever a student of the philosopher; I'm familiar with the quotation because a psychotherapist friend scribbled it out for me on a prescription pad, as if I could take it to the drugstore and get it filled. It was sound advice, but before I could "be with what is," I had to give up what was and could be no more—and that, as my friend well knew, is a painful undertaking for which there is no known palliative.

As part of my job, I began to travel across the country, covering construction projects. I wrote about an interstate highway cutting across the rugged hills of northern Georgia, a skyscraper rising above Lake Huron, a dam slung across the Catawba River, a tunnel in the soft Chesapeake mud. One

191

•

first
you
have
to
row
a
little
boat

day my editor sent me to the Canadian border, where a consortium of contractors was sinking a series of missile silos beside Lake Champlain.

I stood on the brink of one of those silos, more than a hundred feet across, and stared into the huge cavity in the earth's crust. At the bottom of the pit, I could see workmen shoveling rocky debris, the leftovers from a dynamite blast, into a bucket attached to a crane boom. When the bucket was full, the crane—poised like a prehistoric bird on the brim of the silo—raised it to the top and dumped its contents into a truck.

I had heard that a workman had been killed several weeks earlier when a stone tumbled out of an overloaded bucket and landed on the back of his neck. I thought of that unknown man and the irony of his death. There he was, carving a hiding place for a ballistic missile with a warhead that could put an end to life on earth, and he was killed by a small stone falling from a bucket over his head.

The project superintendent handed me a hard hat and asked me whether I wanted to ride the bucket down the shaft for a better look. I had done silly things, stupid things, in the interest of getting a better story, but this invitation I had no trouble turning down. I elected to remain safely on the surface, and, as soon as I finished collecting the information I needed, I drove to the airport and flew home.

It was a short trip and the plane never rose high

193

·

first
you
have
to
row
a
little
boat

in the sky. It flew down the Hudson Valley, following the course of the ancient river, and as it passed over the basaltic cliffs above West Point I realized I had come face-to-face with my own mortality. I lived in a crazy world, a fragile world, a world that might at any moment come crashing down around my head. The mere thought of it should have filled me with a fear and trembling, but it had the opposite effect; it filled me with resolve.

When I arrived home I made a bold announcement. "I'm going to sell the sloop!" I said, dropping my voice an octave to give it the weight of authority. I expected a howl of protest, especially from my children, but the only response came from my older daughter, who wanted to know if I was going to read to them because it was her turn to pick the book.

That weekend, I went to the shipyard and told old man Muncey I wanted to sell the sloop. The following Saturday, a prospective buyer came knocking on my door. He offered me slightly less than she was worth, but I didn't quibble. I wanted her off my hands. The next afternoon I drove by her berth from force of habit and she was gone.

That same year, we sold our house and moved into the Rip Van Winkle hills to the north, where the breeze is landlocked and, in summer, the sweet smell of honeysuckle fills the air. I missed the sudden rise of the morning wind from the barrier beach; I miss it still, but I never once regretted the move. My daily commute to Manhattan was easier, and when the time came to quit my job and start free-lance writing I discovered I was in the right place at the right time. My assignments came mainly from *Reader's Digest* and IBM, both of which made their world headquarters not far from where I lived.

And so it was that in our parting the blue sloop taught me the most valuable lesson of all. I had lived through a cycle of learning and caring, and having learned and cared I had to shed the past so I could begin the cycle over again.

TWENTY

·

WINDS OF MEMORY

·

I wake up each morning three thousand miles from where I learned to sail, and sometimes I hear my boyhood self talking to me out of a dream. I am no older than six, and I am tracing the route from my parents' apartment overlooking the Hudson River to my grandparents' brick house near

Sheepshead Bay, where the sea breeze first entered my bones.

My father owned a green Cadillac touring car, and I can see him driving, my mother beside him, as we flew across the Manhattan Bridge and through Prospect Park to Ocean Parkway, while I sat in the rear seat, the soot and pollen filling my eyes, my ears, my nose. And then, all at once, it was as if we had left the land, and all the noxious odors of the land, and entered another realm. My father made a sharp turn under elevated subway tracks and emerged beside an arm of the sea where the boats were swinging at their moorings and the wind blew clean and free.

It was a brief journey from the West Side of Manhattan to the southerly tip of Brooklyn, but they were two entirely different worlds, and even at that early age I knew which was home for me. One was a harsh place filled with city turmoil; the other, a summer haven filled with sweet sounds of "swing" from a beach bandstand mingling with the ocean breeze and drifting landward. Shep Fields played at that bandstand, so did Ben Bernie, Ted Lewis, and Benny Goodman—and I sat high up on my father's shoulders, gazing over the crowd at the gods of music with their clarinets and slide trombones.

After my parents died, I lived with my grandparents for two years in their seaside home on Irwin Street in Manhattan Beach, and I realize now that it

197
·
first
you
have
to
row
a
little
boat

was there, on the Atlantic shore of Brooklyn, that I first became aware of the shift of the wind to the south and the unmistakable scent of the sea. When my grandmother became too ill to care for me, I moved eastward to another seaside home, this one owned by my aunt and uncle, and it was at that time and in that place that I felt the south wind again, and it played like a familiar chantey against the wind I knew.

I am overwhelmed by the power of remembrance. I do not dwell in this precise and fleeting moment, but in the accumulation of all my moments for as far back as my human memory goes. I am my past, and to deny my past is to deny myself, because the life I lived right up to this ephemeral instant defines who I am. My life is not in me; it is in what I remember, and I do not possess what I remember so much as it possesses me.

It would be easy for me to pass myself off as an orphan in a bid for sympathy, but it wouldn't be true. I am not an isolated individual, an island unto myself, cut off from my forebears; my past and present are a continuum, and it is impossible for me to find the boundary between the two. Now flies by; even as I speak, the now in which I thought I dwelt has slipped away, and the words I uttered a heartbeat ago live only in that mansion of myself called memory.

I remember my mother and my father, my grandmother and my grandfather, my aunt and my uncle, and all the times and places we shared. I remember the blue sloop that came out of the wind; I remember Capt. Harrison Watts, Simmy Baker, Ed Doubrava, Oscar Boehme, and all the other friends and mentors with whom I sailed. I remember the Great South Bay as it was when I was a boy, and all those images are with me still, even though I now live on another coast three thousand miles away.

We like to make this artificial distinction between what is fiction and what is fact, what is make-believe and what is true. But I am always surprised when I consider where I met the people who inhabit my memory and who have influenced the course of my life. I met some in the classroom, some in the office, some in the shipyard, and some in the pages of books I read. David Copperfield and Anna Karenina, Odysseus and Joseph K., Emma Bovary and Sancho Panza are as real to me as my parents, my grandparents, my aunt, my uncle, or any of the characters of my bygone youth who made their livelihood along the Great South Bay.

Practical people see this as a kind of blasphemy. "How can you say that?" they want to know. "David Copperfield and Anna Karenina never existed! Somebody made them up!"

They don't know what they say. When I sit alone in my room or walk by myself by the edge of the sea, I summon up those I wish to be with from my

memory. Some are alive and some are dead and
some sprang full-blown from the genius of authors,
and they are all real to me.

199

•

first
you
have
to
row
a
little
boat

One autumn afternoon I received a phone call
from an old friend who was heading up the Coast
Highway and had gotten as far as Santa Cruz, an
hour from where I live. He suggested we meet for
lunch and I readily agreed. As I drove southward—
mountains to my left, ocean to my right—I antici-
pated the experience that lay ahead.

He had been the first friend I made when I moved
to Bay Shore, and we had often sailed together.
After graduating from college, he found a job in
Los Angeles, where he remained, and although we
exchanged Christmas cards I hadn't seen him since.
But we had grown up in the same place, in the same
era, companions and youthful confidants, and, even
though we had each entered another stage of life, I
assumed our shared past would be a bond between
us, permitting our friendship to pick up where it had
left off.

We found an outdoor table on a broad deck overlooking the Pacific. We sat under a yellow umbrella.
A cool wind blew in from the sea. The ambience
was right, but the mood was wrong. As soon as I
began to talk, I felt the stone wall of his reserve.

I spoke of the past, of what I remembered and
what I missed and how I had come to terms as a man
with the loss I had suffered as a boy. He stiffened,

expressing surprise that I was "still struggling" with matters that had happened so long ago. I told him I wasn't struggling with them; I was savoring them.

"The desire to forget the past," I said, "is a form of suicide."

I must have struck a chord, for he sat silently for a long time, as if he was trying to prime his memory, and then spoke so softly that I could barely hear him.

"I feel cheated."

I was so stunned by his use of the word *cheated* that I found it difficult to respond. When I asked him what he meant, he shook his head. At first I thought he was alluding to his inheritance—that he had not been left as much money as he expected because his father had squandered the family fortune before he died. Then I thought it might be something else, something more ominous, perhaps alcoholism or physical abuse.

He finally said he remembered very little about his boyhood in Bay Shore, and what he did remember was too painful to talk about. I never did discover the source of his anguish because he promptly changed the subject, but later, while returning home, I thought about our conversation and realized he had chosen the right word; he had been cheated. It wasn't that somebody else had cheated him; it was that he was cheating himself by his adamant refusal to accept his past. He was so cut off from his boyhood experiences that he couldn't even remember the smell of the morning wind rising off the barrier beach and blowing across the bay.

201

·

first
you
have
to
row
a
little
boat

I was frustrated and angry; the reunion I wanted, the rapport I sought had not occurred. Where a friendship once existed there was now a void, and I was filled with sadness, knowing I couldn't bring it back to life again. Now *I* felt cheated.

The sun was low in the western sky, and as I pulled off the road to watch it disappear into a fog bank I found myself rummaging through my brain for the opening lines of a poem by Robert Frost titled "My November Guest."

> *My Sorrow, when she's here with me,*
> *Thinks these dark days of autumn rain*
> *Are beautiful as days can be;*
> *She loves the bare, the withered tree;*
> *She walks the sodden pasture lane. . . .*

My Sorrow, she was there with me, and I gave myself the sacred right to mourn, not by forgetting but by remembering; not by suppressing events or pushing them into oblivion but by calling them forth from the tangled roots of memory. I remembered the people and places I knew: the blue sloop pointing into the wind and the friends and mentors with whom I sailed, and I knew that I missed them all.

I think most of us are afraid that if we let ourselves feel our sorrow for the passing of the life that was, we will never regain our composure again. But the fear is misplaced; what should truly frighten us is the possibility that we might lose the power to recall the life we lived, which gives us our connection to ourselves. Our most terrifying diseases aren't the ones that take our life; they're the ones that cast us adrift on an empty sea by depriving us of our memories.

A week, a month, a year went by. I did not hear from my friend again. And then one morning a prevailing wind blew out of the Pacific from the northwest, and I remembered my father's green touring car and the sudden change of air when we reached an arm of the sea. I drove to a sailing club and chartered a boat, tacking into the brisk breeze funneling under the Golden Gate Bridge, churning up whitecaps across the bay.

I sailed around Angel Island, past Tiburon and Sausalito, and headed toward Berkeley with the wind astern. To port, the fortress of Alcatraz; to starboard, under my sail, Coit Tower and the gleaming city herself draped across a hill. I gazed about, thinking how different this bay was from the one I had sailed in my blue sloop so long before. I had moved across a continent, migrated to another place and another time, but I had not left the essence of myself behind. I had sailed as a boy, I had sailed as a man, and I was sailing still.